O Television

Stuart Hood

On Television

Pluto Press

First published in 1980 by Pluto Press,
11-21 Northdown Street, London N1 9BN
Second edition 1983
Third edition 1987, reprinted 1989

Copyright © Stuart Hood, 1980, 1983, 1987

Printed and bound in the United Kingdom by
Billing & Sons Limited, Worcester

ISBN 0-86104-702-8

Contents

For Andrew
who is the greatest

Preface to the First Edition

This book sets out to discuss in an accessible way some of the main topics in the study of mass communications and in particular of television. It also contains a description of the structures and mode of functioning of British (and some other) television. I have tried as far as possible to avoid jargon and the specialised vocabulary of professional debate on such topics as mediation and the relationship of the medium to society. I hope the book may be useful to young people who are asking questions about the role of television, to students beginning to examine the workings of the mass media and to teachers. I hope it may be read too by people who are active in trade unions and in the political parties and groups to the left. Many of them will know from experience how television deals with strikes, demonstrations and the activities of radical groups. This book explains some of the workings of television; the point, however, is to change it.

Preface to the Third Edition

The four years since the last edition of this book have seen Thatcherism increasing its grip on British society with predictable effects on broadcasting. There have been attacks by government on the BBC, intervention by the state to prevent the broadcasting of specific programmes, an increasing number of political appointments to the BBC's Board of Governors. The Corporation has responded with even greater editorial caution and a managerial shake-up. Tighter political control has been accompanied by the loosening of commercial restraints. The IBA has increased the amount of advertising time. There is pressure for Channel 4 to become self-supporting — a step the advertisers hope will lower advertising rates. The effect on programmes if the Channel has to compete for ratings can be guessed. Cable transmissions have been slow to develop. It is on satellites that the financial interests in broadcasting pin their hopes to boost an audience which they define 'as increasingly small, old and downmarket'. Meantime, the BBC did not — as was expected (p.120) venture into satellite broadcasting; insead the IBA have awarded a franchise for Direct Broadcasting by Satellite (DBS) to a consortium which includes Anglia TV, Granada, Pearsons (the publishing group) and Virgin Records. Advertisers foresee 'a 36% penetration of satellite dishes (for reception of DBS) by 1995'.

Throughout Western Europe the drive towards deregulation has continued with the selling-off of French public service channels. Satellite broadcasting is dominated by commercial organisations aiming at a young audience with a staple of pop videos and films.

Public service broadcasting, with its potential to offer a wide range of programmes and provide a genuine public forum, is under attack from many quarters. There is little sign so far of the political will to defend and reform it.

1 The Screen

In most highly developed countries television is as easily available as water, gas or electricity. We can switch all of them on or off at will. Just as we do not wonder where the water, the gas or the electricity come from, how they get to us, or what processes they go through, so we do not generally wonder how television pictures reach our screens. Television pictures tend to be unquestioned; they are accepted as being as 'natural' as gas, water or electricity. They seem to be untouched by human hand. This 'natural' look is so important to the people who choose the pictures on our screens - which they do with the help of very costly and complicated electronic equipment - that they go to great lengths to eliminate any clues to their part in the process of selection. This is one of the reasons why a picture which includes a camera or a microphone is usually avoided, the rule being that they should not, unless in exceptional circumstances, be shown to the viewer. Professional rules of this kind sometimes have good, rational explanations; sometimes they have no such justification, but in either case they will be described by the professionals involved as 'only commonsense'. 'Commonsense' is a word which can conceal important, unstated ideas and assumptions about the purposes of television, about the audience, about the role of the professionals, and about society itself. One of the topics we shall return to in this book is the meaning of 'commonsense' assumptions about television.

Television provides us with a succession of images on the screen. Usually they are accompanied by words, music or sound. Indeed, research has shown that viewers react as much to the sounds - exciting music for instance - as to the pictures. Sound clues are often signals to make the viewers give their full attention to what is going on on their screens. It is because of the importance of the aural signals that the professionals are insistent that the images must always be accompanied by some sort of sound. Lack of sound might mean to the viewers that there was something wrong with their sets. These words, music and sound are employed to tell us how to react to the images on our screens and how to interpret them. But even if the worst were to happen and we were to lose sound, we would still be able to read many of the images. This is possible because we have grown up in a particular society, have gone through a particular educational system, have been exposed to certain key images in certain ways and certain circumstances. In British society a red, white and blue flag is expected to arouse in us feelings of patriotism, thoughts about 'our country', sensations of loyalty to the Crown; and indeed it has this effect in the minds of large numbers of our fellow-citizens. Since it was invented in the early eighteenth century the Union Jack has acquired a range of powerful associations. When it is shown on our television screens we are expected to react in a way that accepts these associations. There are those - including a considerable proportion of programme-makers working for television - who would argue that such associations and their accompanying emotions or ideas are shared by most television audience (which they sometimes equate with 'the public'); that these feelings and ideas belong to the consensus in our society. The concept of the consensus - a body of shared ideas and attitudes - is very important since it lies behind many of the judgements made by programme-makers. It is true that if within a society there were no consensus about certain images or signs, society might find it difficult to function. We all accept that a red light means *Stop* and a green one *Go* and there other neutral signs of this kind. Without such a consensus we would not be able to read the messages of the traffic signals. As members of one society we may not be able to read the signs of another society. An Indian totem pole with its intricate carved designs is to most of us merely an object of beauty and interest; we cannot read the message of the images carved in the wood. We can, however, within our own culture, easily read the quick succession of images that precedes the main ITN (Independent Television News) newscast. Here the shot of the earth from space indicates the global coverage of the ITN news service; the stills of great capital cities point to ITN's global coverage of news; and the final shot - the dial of Big Ben - suggests the importance of the institution of parliament and implies that the newscast shares the accuracy of the nation's time-piece.

Naturally in a politically divided society not everyone will react to the Union Jack with the required responses. There are a range of dissenting reactions to it. The consensus reading is presented in such a way by the medium, however, that it attempts to disregard and override dissident readings. It is the essence of the idea of a consensus that it attempts, at a conscious and unconscious level, to impose the view that there is only one 'right' reading. Dissenting readings should be rejected by the audience. This assumption derives from the view that we - that is the audience and the broadcaster - are united in one nation in spite of class or political divisions. The broadcasters present their images to the public with all the authority of the great public organisations for which they work. The 'public' is expected to accept the proposed reading without question. But images are in themselves nearly all open to a variety of inter-pretations. Does a shot of a young man or woman in a camouflage uniform and holding an automatic rifle represent a soldier, a freedom fighter, a guerilla or a terrorist? The picture can carry any one of these readings. A picture of workers out-side a factory may suggest to the active trade unionists that they are pickets, workers engaged in a struggle with which they sympathise. But there are other readings which include 'troublemakers', 'extremists', 'dissidents', 'disruptive elements'. In cases like this - or in the case of the young man or woman with the rifle - the broadcasters will find it necessary to tell us how we should read the image. This they do by the choice of the word they put alongside the picture; the word fixes it - anchors it. We, as members of the public, are expected to accept that the word really does fit the image. The choice of the 'right' word is an important editorial and political decision. We shall decribe later the basis on which these decisions are made.

There are other important messages to be got from the images on our screens, even without the addition of sounds or words. If you take note, over a period of time, of which people are allowed to talk directly to the viewers - looking straight at the camera and so straight out of the screen - you will find that they constitute a small and carefully defined group. They include station announcers (who tell us what programmes are to be shown or what changes have been made in the evening's schedules), weather forecasters, programme presenters whose job is to introduce speakers and outline the nature of, say, a discussion programme; and they include the newscasters. All these persons have one thing in common. They are there to give us information which we are asked to assume is accurate (as indeed some of it is), unbiased and authoritative (which it is less likely to be). They have authority vested in them by the television organisations and can be described in a useful phrase as 'bearers of truth'. But there is another and more interesting category. It includes the monarch, the prime minister, cabinet ministers when they make official broadcasts (what are called ministerial broadcasts) and the leader of the parliamentary opposition front bench, who is allowed in certain circumstances to reply to a ministerial broadcast if the broadcasting authorities judge that it was controversial. All these persons - and one or two others including the Archbishop of Canterbury as head of the Church of England - are allowed to address the television audience ('the public' or 'the nation' as the broadcasters call it on such occasions) directly. They do so by reason of their constitutional or political authority. On other occasions - for instance when the Chancellor of the Exchequer is interviewed about the Budget - they are all (with the exception of the Queen) treated like ordinary people; that is to say, they are shown in profile or in such a way that their gaze is not fixed directly on the viewers but on the interviewer who is with them in the studio. In other words their statements have to pass through someone else, as it were - they have to be mediated. If they attempt to take on the role of a person of authority and address an audience directly, the director will cut away from them and go back to a shot of the interviewer. This has been known to happen to a senior politician who broke the conventions of the studio situation - one in which he was being interrogated not being invited to address the public at large - and looked at the camera. There are, however, certain politically unimportant persons who *are* allowed to address the camera directly - people like comedians, who are the equivalent of medieval jesters and, like the jesters, are allowed to act as if they had the same privileges as the men and women of power in our society. For that is what the full face picture means: that the man or woman on the screen has power and authority.

As a footnote to this analysis of the images of power on our screens it can be argued that television is doing no more in this case than continue a convention which goes back in the history of Western art to those early religious paintings in which certain figures from Christian teaching - God the Father, Christ and the Virgin Mary - were always shown full face because they were considered to be precisely 'bearers of truth'. Ordinary human beings like the shepherds or kings in pictures of the Nativity, or the donors of the painting came to be shown in profile. So important was this distinction that in early Spanish painting there was a portrait of the Virgin which was condemned as heretical because it showed her in profile - as if she were a mere human being. The power of this convention makes it all the more remarkable that in his *Adoration of the Virgin*, Botticelli painted his own portrait staring out of the canvas at the viewer, while the great Florentine nobility are duly reverential and shown in profile.

There are other important conventions which govern the kind of picture we see on our screens. They have to do with the way people are framed - that is to say, the kind of shot that film or television cameramen take of their subjects. The convention is that in 'factual' programmes they should be shot from eye-level and not from above or below, since shots from either of these angles would present an image slanted in more senses than one. The other convention deals with the question of how 'tight' a shot may be. Generally, important figures will be shown in medium close-up which shows them from the waist up. This may be replaced by a close-up which shows only the subject's head and shoulders. It would be very rare for a big close-up - a shot showing only the head - to be used of an important person. Just as in our normal social intercourse we observe certain conventions about how close we come to other people and how close we allow them to come to us, so when choosing their images, television cameras keep a certain distance from their subjects. There is around us all an imaginary space which we might define as the sphere of intimacy - kissing distance, so to speak - which only certain persons in certain roles are normally allowed to penetrate. This space is generally respected by TV cameras. It is almost inconceivable that one should see on the television screen a big close-up of a figure of authority - of a prime minister or international statesman. The camera stands back from them. But in the case of ordinary people it is not unknown for the camera to come close in, particularly if the subject is in a state of emotional excitement, grief or joy. Sportsmen and women, although important and prestigious national figures, can be shown weeping or winning an award for 'their country'; they, too, are only human.

You will look in vain in the handbooks of television direction or in the 'grammars' of film and television for a discussion of the way subjects should be shot in studio or on location which deals with the question in the terms used here. In manuals dealing with the direction of television cameras the framing of shots is certainly discussed, but always in terms of aesthetics and of

Do's and *Don'ts*, which one is not expected to question. It is in these terms that camera crews or directors discuss the problem, falling back if necessary on the argument that it is all a matter of 'commonsense'. What they are unwilling to recognise is that the framing of a picture on the screen or the setting that is chosen for a subject can be of more than aesthetic importance; that it can be an indication of how we should react to the subject presented on the screen; and that an aesthetic judgement can conceal a political one. Thus a cameraman filming the memorial to the victims of Bloody Sunday in Derry was observed to frame the shot in such a way as to avoid an unaesthetic gap on either side of the monument - a gap which would have been filled with distracting activity from passers-by. Tight framing did, it is true, cut out external activity, but it also eliminated an inscription below the official one, an inscription added by the IRA to commemorate the 'victims of British imperialism'. A more obvious example of how the choice of images indicates what our attitude to the persons in shot should be is provided by the stock picture of pickets outside a factory gate. When they are interviewed the camera is frequently hand-held; the picture will probably include a considerable amount of extraneous activity; those who are interviewed find themselves in a situation which is difficult to control. By contrast the representatives of the employers are usually shot in their offices surrounded by the paraphernalia of power and authority, having had the chance - if only while the lighting equipment was being installed and the camera-tripod set up - to consider what they want to say. It is, however, not necessary in such cases for us to be able to hear what is being said to know which of the two subjects we are expected to find more authoritative. Such visual messages have an important content - a connotation which includes assumptions concerning the status of certain individuals and classes in society and their relative power positions. The images on our television screens are the means - along with other media such as the press, books and (less importantly) film - of conveying an ideology: that view of society which has been evolved to provide a seemingly rational and therefore unquestionable explanation of how it works and of the power relationships within it. If, however, you put this view of the function of television and its images to the professionals who manufacture them they will be politely ironical and reply that, on the contrary, the images are chosen on the basis of judgements which are 'natural' or 'commonsense'. But as Gramsci, the Italian revolutionary, remarked: 'Commonsense is the sense of the ruling class'.

Those images which are selected to appear on our television screens are obviously only a tiny sample of the infinite choice offered by the world around us. Those which are chosen fall into two categories: those which reflect what is called 'actuality', that is to say, events which are happening as we see them on our sets (or which happened fairly recently); and those which belong to the realm of fiction, such as the actions in a play or film. Those in the first category are sometimes seen as being what marks television off from all the other representational arts, such as film, drawing or painting, or photography, in that the pictures offered by television are 'live'. Through them we see events as they occur. Examples vary from an international tennis tournament to a state occasion or to a television spectacular like man's first moon landing: a show mounted to demonstrate to a worldwide audience the United States' supremacy in space. What happens when an event is shown live is that the director in charge of the broadcast makes from minute to minute a selection from an array of pictures offered by a number of television cameras and presented simultaneously on monitors. Out of this multiplicity of images he or she composes, as the event unrolls, an account of what is happening - a story with a beginning, a middle and an end. It is a task requiring great presence of mind, quick reactions and a firm grasp of the requirements of the programme into which the images will be fed. Thus in covering a football match directors are unlikely to include pictures which suggest that the game is boring. They cannot, for example, begin to look around at what is going on in the street outside or study the behaviour of the crowd. It requires something very dramatic indeed to make them abandon the game altogether and turn the cameras elsewhere. An example of such a situation occurred during the Munich Olympics when the cameras switched from the events in the stadium to show the police action against the Palestinian commandos who had attacked the Israeli contingent.

As is the case with many other judgements that go to shape television programmes, decisions about which pictures can be shown and which rejected have to be made on the spur of the moment. That is why the professionals involved have to make the - mostly unwritten - rules which govern matters of 'taste' and of political decision so much a part of their way of thinking that they can make 'correct' judgements without reflection. It is said that one question put to a candidate for a post in the BBC's outside broadcast department was this: 'You are covering (live) the

Queen's departure from London Airport. The plane takes off but fails to gain height and crashes at the end of the runway. Do you stay with the blazing plane or do you cut away from it and if so to what?' The example, if true, illustrates two things: the BBC's obsession with royalty and the real problem of how much should be shown of a crash, of mangled bodies, of extremes of grief and pain, of a man or woman's last moments. These are all questions of 'taste'; but 'taste' is socially determined. There are societies where executions are public and are filmed for television. Television directors are expected to know what their society - or the controlling authorities in it - finds acceptable. It would be perfectly possible to shoot a royal occasion, some piece of medieval pomp, in such a way to make it an explicit comment on the close links between the monarchy and the military establishment or to penetrate behind the pageantry to the relationships of class and wealth which they so picturesquely camouflage. But it is difficult to imagine any existing society allowing its figures of authority and power to be publicly questioned in this way on television, which in most cases is either state-licensed or state-controlled.

The process of choosing certain pictures and rejecting others is an example of what is often described as 'gate-keeping'. The figure of speech is taken from the way in which a farmer stands at the door of a pen and by moving a gate from side to side as the cattle or sheep pass through separates them out for dipping, for the market or the slaughterhouse. Gate-keeping is an essential part of the function of any editor. In the case of television outside broadcasts, as we have seen, gate-keeping takes place as the events unroll; but the very fact that the broadcast is taking place is the result of gate-keeping at another level, in the shape of the editorial decision to cover that particular event rather than some other of more or less equal interest and importance. Here the words 'interest' and 'importance' - 'important' to whom? 'interesting' to whom? - seem on the face of it simple but in reality they conceal a number of complicated assumptions about the audience and its interests and about the role of television in society.

Naturally the same sort of gate-keeping decisions are made when deciding what film should be shown in a television newscast or in a current affairs programme. But in this case the chain of editorial decisions is longer and the number of gate-keepers therefore larger. Suppose there is a strike in a small factory in an industrial town in the North of England. News of the strike may first come to the attention of a local reporter - a 'stringer' - who has professional film equipment necessary to provide news coverage for the local television station from time to time. The first decision is whether the story is worth covering. In making it reporters will probably look for some factor that distinguishes the situation from the normal run of strikes: such as that there are a lot of black or Asian workers involved, or a lot of women, or that a section of the work force opposes the strike, or (better still) that some of the strikers' wives are said to oppose their husbands' actions. They may then go off to shoot some footage of the situation, probably after clearing with the local television newsroom that they are interested in the story. On arriving at the factory they will once again decide whether what they find there is 'interesting' or 'important' enough to shoot. Here the criteria will include the number of pickets, the level of police activity, the number of blacklegs crossing the picket line, whether there are demonstrations by wives or any other manifestation which marks the occasion as being in some way different from and more 'interesting' than a normal strike. The degree of 'interest' increases if there are incidents between strikes and the police; between strikers and scabs; between housewives and strikers. Having shot the footage, the stringer will get it to the local newsroom where a news-editor will view it and decide whether it merits inclusion in the local newscast. This too will be decided on the basis of 'interest' and 'importance'. If it is considered 'very interesting' or 'very important', the London newsroom will be informed and the pictures will be sent there electronically by underground cable. On arrival they will be examined by the London news-editor along with a great deal of other material on industrial disputes and included in the national bulletin on the basis of 'interest' and 'importance'. In the case of news-stories from abroad the same criteria are applied; the only difference is that the chain of gate-keepers is longer, stretching from, say, the camera crew of an international news film agency in East Africa by way of the agency's editorial staff to the gate-keepers in the BBC or ITN. An incident in Latin America, in India, in Africa or anywhere else in the Third World, has to be very remarkable before it is judged 'interesting' or 'important'; which usually means either that a high degree of human suffering is involved or else that the interests of the developed world are directly threatened.

So far we have talked mainly in terms of pictures because it is important to understand that they have a power and a meaning that is independent of words. They are, however, as we have seen, often given precise meaning only when a word is attached to them. It is interesting to see, for instance, how rebels against colonial power are described in hostile terms until they achieve independence, when the terms applied to them are altered. During the struggle for independence in Zimbabwe, Robert Mugabe, the guerilla commander, was described, both in his own country's and in the British media, in negative and abusive terms; when it became clear that, in an independent Zimbabwe, important British interests were not threatened, he ceased to be called a rebel or terrorist leader and was described in terms of respect appropriate for the leader of a new nation. Words reflect the realities of political relationships and political power. Changes in the words used to describe particular politicians and political groups reflect the judgements of the news organisations as to their standing. A very obvious case is that of the IRA, which carries out operations indistinguishable from those of the various resistance movements supported by the allies during the Second World War. The members of these movements were described in the allied press and radio as heroes, and by the press of the regimes against which they fought as 'bandits', 'assassins' or 'gangsters'; today the British press and the British media use a range of words from 'bastards' to 'terrorists' to describe the IRA. The words spoken to accompany the pictures on our screens have been as carefully chosen and sifted as the images. Once again there is a chain of gate-keepers, running from the reporter or correspondent who writes the first story to the editor who looks at the final story and alters a word here and there. We shall discuss later how the men and women in the process of gate-keeping know what words to use and how to judge whether a story is 'interesting' or 'important' and how they come to know when their judgements are correct.

Closely connected with the process of gate-keeping is the function known as 'agenda-setting'. This is a term used to describe the way in which those who work in the medium of television (and also of radio or of the press) set the context within which a topic of public interest is discussed on the air and in front of the cameras. The process can typically begin off-screen when the producer responsible for a programme like *Panorama* or *Nationwide* discusses with the person who is to conduct an interview what questions should be put to the inter-viewee, whether that person is a politician, a trade unionist, a celebrity of some kind, or merely a member of the public who has suddenly and briefly become 'news'. Between them they will decide what ground should be covered in the interview and will go over the main questions to be put during the broadcast. On one level this is a sensible and practical ('commonsense') step to take so as to prevent the discussion from wandering or running out of time. (Both considerations, of course, contain unspoken assumptions about the attention span of the audience and the nature of human discourse). But it can also be a way of refusing to discuss certain aspects of a topic and of steering the discussion away from difficult areas. 'We don't want to get into that', is the sort of comment that is likely to be heard when some angle is discussed that does not fit into the general scheme of the interview, is believed not to be 'interesting' or not suitable for discussion. Often a similar conversation will take place with the interviewee, particularly if he or she is politically important. 'We thought we ought to cover the following points', the interviewer may typically say - the incorporation of the interviewee in the 'we' being in this context a very important trick of language and one that makes it more difficult for the interviewee to refuse to agree with the proposal. It is, of course, always open to the interviewee at this point to suggest other areas for discussion; but unless he or she is very persuasive or very powerful (in the sense of possessing social or political weight), it is unlikely that the interviewer will accept the counter-proposals.

Another form of agenda-setting can sometimes be observed on the screen. It is marked by such interventions by the interviewer as: 'May I bring you back to the point we were dealing with earlier?' (the courtesy in the formula is purely formal for this is in fact an order) or 'Perhaps we might look at that another time - tonight, however, I think we ought to concentrate on ... ' In very difficult cases, when the interviewee persists in trying to push his or her own line or obstinately produces answers at variance from those the interview was designed to elicit, the interview may be brought to a summary close by the device of 'And now I hand you' (that is to say, the audience) 'back to Bill Bloggs. Bill!' It is very rare to see an interviewee succeed in pushing the conversation in a direction other than that planned by the interviewer and the producer. In order to do so interviewees must have thought out beforehand exactly what they wish to say; they must be fluent and determined and must be prepared to appear 'awkward' on the air in front of the television cameras. It requires considerable experience of handling an interview situation and the kind of authority discussed above.

Thus, when at the end of the 1979 Labour Party Conference, Callaghan was interviewed by Robin Day and asked whether he had not suffered a defeat over the proposals for party reform and whether as a consequence he ought to consider resigning from the leadership of the party, Callaghan used his political status - and his familiarity with the medium - to refuse to answer Day's questions. His ability to turn the tables on Day was acknowledged by the director in an interesting way - which refers back to what was said earlier about the significance of the image on the screen and what it can tell us. At the end of the interview viewers would normally expect to have seen the cameras cut to Day who would wind up the interview and thank the interviewee. On this occasion something unusual happened. Callaghan was in shot, having refused for the second or third time to answer Day's question about retirement; when he finished speaking the camera stayed on him and from off-screen Day could be heard apologising for his 'journalistic impetuosity' - an apology which Callaghan (still in shot) graciously accepted. There the interview ended with Day eclipsed and invisible and Callaghan victorious in shot. It was an interesting television moment.

One of the main purposes of agenda-setting is to avoid a discussion from opening out and placing the topic in hand in a wider context than the interviewer had planned. This is in line with the approach common to most television and radio interviewers who try to avoid contextualisation because it can raise questions which the interviewer or the producer may neither be willing nor indeed equipped to deal with. An attempt by a hospital worker to make the point that cuts in the health service are part of a general attempt to dismantle the welfare state and that they are parallelled by cuts in education and other social services, is likely to be interrupted by the interviewer with a remark such as 'I must bring you back to the subject - what we are discussing are hospital closures not the social services as a whole'. There are a number of reasons why interviewers adopt such tactics. They may not have researched the wider question of the cuts sufficiently to be confident that they can handle the situation in the sense that they may not feel able to achieve 'balance' by asking (in accordance with a long-established practice) questions which 'put the other side'. (Here it has to be borne in mind that television interviewers, who are in general well informed, have to work under great pressure on occasions and may have rather short notice of the kind of interview they will be required to undertake.) They too are subject to strains and stresses, and have to be careful not to embarrass their immediate superiors or the organisation for which they work. This is one reason - not the only reason nor indeed the most important reason - why they tend to grasp at any safe formulation. Thus it has been noticeable that the question of inflation has for long been discussed on television almost exclusively in terms of 'excessive wage demands', which are assumed to be its main cause. This is a safe angle to pursue, for the theory that inflation is caused by rising wages is widely diffused in the broadcasting media and in the press. It has become part of the conventional wisdom of both journalists and politicians. Wage demands are then linked with 'disruptive strikes', which are put forward as a main reason for the bad economic situation of the country, no account being taken of the deficiencies of management or the general crisis of capitalism itself. A Glasgow University team which made a study of this type of agenda-setting demonstrated how it works in such cases. In an interview recorded off-air by the Glasgow team, a shop stewards' convenor at Cowley pointed out to the interviewer that most stoppages at the plant did not result from industrial action and that 'most of the production had been lost through either breakdowns or shortage of materials'. Unperturbed by this information (which did not fit into his 'agenda'), the interviewer proceeded to ask what the shop steward thought of the prospect of no government financial support for the undertaking 'if the strike record doesn't improve'. In other words, because the shop steward's reply did not suit the 'agenda', the interviewer overrode it and tried to get the discussion back into a direction that coincided with his own assumptions.

There are other more direct controls over what goes out from the studio and ends up on our television screens. Here the central figure is the director sitting in the control gallery and following the flow of events in the studio below him on an array of monitors. Directors have the final say about what the viewer sees because they not only choose the pictures as the interview develops but can decide to leave one studio situation and go over to another if it appears that the interview has gone on too long, has ceased to be 'interesting' or is becoming in some way difficult. They are in constant contact with the interviewers through the little, unobtrusive microphone which the latter wear and, through it, can give instructions to move on to another topic, to press the interview on a particular point or to bring the interview to an end. Control of the situation is often facilitated by the geography of the studio - the way in which sets are distributed or the physical distances between (say) an anchorman, a panel of experts and a studio audience drawn from 'the public'. If they are some distance apart, members of the audience can find that they are too far from the other participants for normal conversational exchanges; in that case they must wait for the microphone to be offered to them. It can also be withdrawn if a member of the audience is obstreperous, asks awkward questions or otherwise breaks the rules of studio behaviour; the cameras will then switch to the panel or the anchorman who can usually be relied on to observe the conventions.

Agenda-setting is of more than academic interest - it is also something which you can learn to observe as you watch studio interviews. By studying the way it works members of the public who are likely in the course of political activity to find themselves in front of a television camera can develop counter-strategies. Many politicians have developed such techniques; a common one is to say: 'Before answering that question (that interesting question) may I just say ... ' They then proceed to make the one point which they intended to put across when they agreed to be interviewed. It is not for nothing that the main political parties and important interest groups within society give their members training in interviewing techniques in television studios where they acquire the skills of the game. Members of the political groups which lie outside the parliamentary consensus are not likely to have the same training facilities or to be treated with the same consideration. The rules of interviewing are in that sense unfair. Some organisations on the left respond to the unequal rules by refusing to appear at all on television unless they have complete control of the situation. This is possible only in two circumstances: one of these is a general election political party broadcast for which a party qualifies only if it puts fifty or more candidates in the field. In the case of a small party the cost of putting up fifty or more deposits in order to have air-time makes the resulting broadcast an exceedingly expensive commercial. The other is an access programme, like the *Open Door* programme mounted by a Southall group to express their views on police brutality during the anti-National Front demonstration in which Blair Peach was killed. Outside such situations a number of precautions can be taken. One is to insist in the case of a news interview that it takes place in circumstances and surroundings that give the interviewees the greatest possible psychological advantage - in an office and not on the pavement, in some surrounding where they feel at ease. In studio situations anyone who agrees to take part must be absolutely clear before entering the studio about what points require to be made and should resist all efforts by the interviewer to set the agenda. Above all interviewees must be prepared to counter-attack. When very highly paid interviewers suggest that 'we - the members of the public' are fed up with demands from low-paid workers for a wage rise, they should be asked what their take-home pay is; if asked - as happened on *Nationwide* in the autumn of 1979 - 'You are a trade unionist - doesn't this mean that you are politically motivated?' the interviewee should enquire whether the interviewer is a trade union member and what his or her motives are. Members of groups likely to be interviewed should study the media, practise interviewing techniques and get in touch with people in the media who have the knowledge and willingness to help.

2 The Audience

Most people are unlikely ever to find themselves in front of film or television cameras in a studio or elsewhere, although the chances of being recorded by police video equipment in the course of a demonstration or picket are now quite high. They will remain anonymous members of the audience for television, of 'the public' - two terms which are sometimes used on television as if they were the same thing. The concept of 'the audience' is obviously important for the television professionals, as it is indeed for anyone who is engaged in the business of communication. In the case of television, it is particularly important because of special nature of the television audience. A lecturer or politician at a public meeting can see and gauge the size of their audience; a newspaper editor has a return of sales which gives a measurable approximation to the size of the readership; but the television professional often has a desperate feeling that the programme just broadcast, on which a great deal of time and energy has been spent, may have been both unseen and unheard. This feeling of panic is allayed by the flicker of screens which the person who made the programme will see on the way home from the television studio. Yet how many of these sets were turned on to this particular programme? What was its audience? There are figures available but they take some time to obtain. These figures are - even at their smallest - very large. Thus a Christmas Day programme with Morecambe and Wise was said to have an audience of 29 million; an 'access' programme in which members of the public are allowed to state their own views (a rare event), had a mere 750,000 - a figure which, in terms of any other medium (press, publishing or film), would be enormous. These figures are statistical estimates obtained, in the case of the BBC, by a continuous survey of viewers and listeners in the course of which almost a million people are interviewed during any one year. In the case of commercial television, they are obtained by monitoring the readings provided by automatic electronic meters attached to sets in a representative sample of 2,622 homes. The two methods are different and give different results. BBC audience research tends to produce audience figures more favourable to BBC television, whereas the monitoring of sets carried out on behalf of commercial television tends to favour ITV. If questioned on this discrepancy, the researchers will not criticise the work of their colleagues in the rival organisation. It is simply, they say, that they are measuring different things and using different methods to do so. This does not prevent the managements and public relations officers of the rival organisations from exploiting the differing results to their own advantage. What is clear is that there are, in both methods, built-in weaknesses of which the audience researchers are perfectly aware. In the case of the BBC's face-to-face interviews, of which it conducts a quota of between 2,000 and 2,500 daily, there is the danger that the interviewee will be anxious to please someone who represents the BBC, a prestigious national institution; to this must be added the genuine difficulty some interviewees have in remembering whether the programme they saw was this week's or last week's, yesterday's or the day before's. In the case of commercial television, there is the obvious problem that the electronic meter shows only that the set was switched on to a particular time and not how many people were actually viewing. If we take a family of four - two parents and two children - the pattern of viewing may be that, in the early evening, there are four people in front of the set; the children will go to bed at their respective bedtimes and the parents may retire together or one may stay on watching until close-down, so that over the evening the number of viewers in the family decreases. These are recognisable defects for which allowance can be made by the reseachers. But the fundamental problem connected with viewing figures is not so much such distorting factors as the use made of them and the assumptions based on them by their users.

On one level, audience figures can be used by the television professionals who make the programmes and those who schedule them to spot those cases where there is a difference between the size of the audience, as determined by audience research, and their own expectation of how many viewers the programme might attract. For example, if what is intended as a popular programme - that is one designed to attract a large audience - has few viewers it clearly has not fulfilled the programme-makers' expectations. Either it did not appeal to the viewers or it was poorly executed or there was very strong opposition on the other channels. According to their reading of the situation the professsionals can decide to alter the content and format of the programme, to replace it with another programme or to move it to a place in the schedule where the opposition is less damaging. If, on the other hand, what was conceived as a minority programme attracts a large audience there is something about the nature of the programme which needs to be examined. This is what happened in the sixties when the first 'satirical' programmes were scheduled late at night for what was presumed to be a small, sophisticated audience, but in fact attracted a very large one. The explanation was that the programmes had expressed a widely felt sense of disrespect for certain establishment figures and attitudes - a disrespect which was shared by a much wider section of the public than the programme-makers had even guessed.

Audience figures or ratings, as they are called, are used in this way by programme planners and programme-makers in both BBC and commercial television. It is a use of statistics which conceals a number of assumptions about audiences and about the nature of programmes: what is a 'popular' programme, for example? How do the programme-makers know what is 'popular' and what is not? But in the case of commercial televison the ratings have a further and more obvious use. Commercial television has been accurately described as a system of broadcasting whereby an audience is delivered (as the technical expression goes) to an advertiser, the programme being the bait to attract the audience to watch the advertisements that go out in programme breaks. The advertiser judges the usefulness of advertising on television by how much it costs him to buy the attention of each thousand viewers as measured by audience research: this figure is called 'the cost per thousand'. The concept of the cost per thousand is central to the running of a commercial television network. Since the advertisers obviously want the cost per thousand to be as low as possible, there is a strong incentive for commercial television companies to obtain the largest possible audiences. Too high a cost per thousand may make the advertiser switch to some other medium such as radio or the press and thus deprive the commercial television of part of its essential income. This system is seen working in its extreme form in American commercial television where the competition between the three main networks for the audience and for the advertising revenue is intense. In most western European countries, because of the excesses of the American model, safeguards have been built into the broadcasting systems which control the amount of advertising and thus prevent the all-out pursuit of ratings. In Britain, for instance, the amount of advertising is limited to three minutes per programme hour and the business interests represented by the commercial television companies find themselves unable to enjoy the absolutely free play of the market forces which would, if unrestrained, push for the maximum audience at all times. This does not mean they have not made huge profits.

Sometimes the advertisers are not satisfied with mere numbers. The audience delivered to them must be of the right kind - that is, composed of the kind of person who has the purchasing power to buy the products advertised in the commercial breaks. There have been cases - notably in the United States - where programmes have been taken off, not because the audience for them was small, but because it contained too many old or too many young viewers, viewers who were unlikely to be able to go out and buy the goods advertised on their screens. The importance of the composition of the audience and its potential spending-power is illustrated by an argument which was put forward during the discussion over the opening of the second commercial channel in Britain - the so-called Fourth Channel. Here it has been suggested that advertisers might be willing to accept smaller audiences than those obtained by ITV provided that their spending power was high. That is to say, if the audience were to be what has been described as a 'a Sunday colour supplement audience', lower ratings might be acceptable. The cost per thousand would then be high but the audience, considered as a market, would be rich.

Why should ratings also be important - as they are - for a public service organisation like the BBC, which has no commercial reason to maximise audiences and so - on the face of it - need not worry about the cost per thousand? The answer is that the size of the BBC's audience is of political importance. We shall have to look later at the relationship between the BBC and the centres of political power; all that it is necessary to understand at this point is that the BBC depends for its income on the licence fees paid by viewers and that the size of this licence is determined by government, which at various times in the history of the BBC has arbitrarily withheld a proportion of the licence revenue - 16 per cent of it in the 1950s, for example. So long as the BBC enjoyed a broadcasting monopoly this dependence on government, though irksome, was accepted by the BBC as a fact of life; its position as a national institution was very secure and the question of how large an audience it attracted was not a political issue, although there were voices on the Tory side which pointed to the large number of listeners attracted to the commercial broadcasts of Radio Luxembourg - particularly on Sundays when the pre-war BBC's puritanical policies forbade the broadcasting of entertainment programmes. The situation changed with the coming of commercial television in 1955 and with the transfer to the television studios of the commercial companies of precisely some of the most popular radio programmes broadcast by Radio Luxembourg. After a shaky start commercial television attracted a large and growing audience. Soon there was evidence from audience research that the BBC was capable of attracting only a third or less of the available viewers. It was at this point that the ratings became politically important. A BBC executive has recorded in her memoirs a conversation she had at this time with a junior minister who made it clear that if the BBC's share of the audience falls to as low as 20 per cent 'the government could not possibly insist that the BBC's licence fee should continue to be paid. Politically it would be impossible to ask 80 per cent of the viewing public to pay for the benefits enjoyed by only 20 per cent.' The support for commercial television from MPs on both sides of the House of Commons brought home to the BBC that unless its share of the audience increased - unless it could demonstrate that it was an efficient and lively broadcasting organisation - it would be difficult for it to approach government for an increase in the licence fee at any future date. The decision was therefore taken in the early sixties to attempt to increase the BBC's share of the audience to around 50 per cent if possible without lowering the standard of programmes. The attempt succeeded during the boom period of the sixties, but the BBC found itself in a difficult situation again in the seventies, when the pressures of inflation eroded its revenue. How that situation affected its relationship to government we shall see later.

There were other forces at play within the BBC which favoured a competitive attitude expressed in figures of its share of the television audience. One of these was rivalry between television professionals anxious to be able to measure their personal success in attracting large audiences. Ratings were the only relatively solid evidence of such success, although what the figures did not, of course, reveal was how successful the programme-makers had been in *communicating* with their audiences. As the competition between the BBC and the commercial television companies increased and as a growing number of freelances began to cross from one network to another as opportunity and their prestige took them, the ability to attract high ratings became a matter of professional pride. In a society where competitiveness is seen as a virtue it is not surprising that it should be fostered in that society's television organisations. Meanwhile, at managerial levels, ratings came to be used to justify executive decisions. Here the questions asked were of this kind: If the audience is (in television terms) very small, how can the employment on programme X of expensive capital equipment and highly paid staff be justified? or What is the smallest audience that a television organisation can afford (in terms the accountants will understand) to transmit to? Thus ratings have come, like any other marketing statistics, to be used in shaping boardroom decisions. Competition has become institutionalised. Success in attracting large audiences is seen as a victory for the organisation which transmitted the programmes. Audience figures are a source of prestige and pride at personal, departmental and institutional levels.

One of the dangers of the ratings is that they can lead to regarding the audience as a homogeneous whole. Yet other kinds of audience research, provided by panels of viewers who record their reactions to particular programmes, provide strong reasons to believe that, if there is an audience of 10 million for a programme, then the reactions of that audience will cover a scale that varies from satisfaction through indifference to rejection. In other words, a large section of the audience may be watching it simply as part of the evening's unbroken flow of moving images because there is no more attractive alternative. Those who reject the programme, on the other hand, may continue to watch precisely because they dislike what they see or because they wish to react to it with critical comments, disrespect for the speakers and so on. The diversity of the audience and the variety of its reactions to programmes is extremely important when it comes to discussing the social and political effects of television. In the earliest discussions of audience reactions, it was suggested that an audience would react to the stimulus of a broadcast message, which in those days was a radio programme, in much the same way as a rat in a laboratory reacts to an electrical shock. It was a theory which bore the marks of the American school of behaviourist psychology. The view that a stimulus provokes a predictable reflex in the audience is one explanation for the immense importance attached to the broadcasting of propaganda during the Second World War and to the battle of words which is still being conducted by the great powers by means of radio (soon, no doubt, to be supplemented by satellite broadcasts of television programmes). The fact is, however, that, even in war-time and even under dictatorships, large numbers of people learn to 'read' the propaganda offered to them at home and from abroad. This skill in reading enables them to interpret correctly such expressions as 'a rectification of the front', which was the German euphemism for a withdrawal, or to know that repeated references to 'our glorious troops' in Italian communiques usually heralded a defeat of these same troops. This does not mean that allied propaganda was accepted without scepticism. Official utterances, wherever their origin, were tested against other information such as reports from soldiers home on leave, from persons who might have special knowledge of events, from conversations with other members of the community, observation of troop movements etc.; they were then interpreted in the light of the listeners' experience, political views, personal hopes and fears.

Something of the same sort goes on when it comes to the public's reading of the messages transmitted by television in the very different conditions of peace-time in a bourgeois democracy. Here the people who formulate the messages - the programme-makers - are not usually involved in the conscious production of propaganda statements. Indeed they will very often deny that what they put on the screen is in any way 'political' - by which they understand some overt statement of a political viewpoint; to them what they transmit represents a commonsense interpretation of events in the world and in their own society. This view they encode in images and words and transmit as a television message. The members of the audience are expected to watch the screen and not only decode the message correctly but to agree with it because they share media people's commonsense view of society. Or such would be the process in a perfect world. What is called 'the preferred reading' would be unquestioningly accepted - a pessimistic thought which is sometimes shared on the left by those who seem to believe that the messages of television must inevitably dominate the minds of the viewers. It is a view of the workings of the mass media which can provide no explanation for the wave of strikes of the winter of 1978-79, when the anti-trade union views explicitly expressed on television by such programmes as *Nationwide* did not prevent large sections of workers from going on strike and for holding out for a very long time. This can only mean that a considerable part of the television audience rejected the 'preferred reading' of the events they saw pictured on their screens and judged both the events and the television representation of them in the light of their own experience as workers and trade unionists - in the light of their class consciousness. When the programme-makers talked of 'the public' and claimed that 'the public' did not approve of the strikes, a section of the audience refused to accept that reading of the situation. They bracketed themselves out of 'the public' into which television attempted to incorporate them.

The fact is that while the programme-makers make important assumptions about their audience they have considerable difficulty in discovering how it reacts to the messages which are constantly being transmitted to it. Such information as they have comes from a variety of sources. Over and above figures of audience size, audience research provides data on how members of the audience enjoyed programmes - what is called the appreciation index: did they enjoy it a lot? a little? moderately? The results of such research is of dubious value, partly because the panels are small and tend to be unrepresentative, partly because the index attempts to quantify subjective judgements of a complicated nature. Then there are viewers' letters, which have to be treated with particular caution. The reasons which prompt members of the public to write to institutions like the BBC or the commercial television companies are very varied. In some sad cases the letters are clearly a cry for help or written from a deep need to have someone to talk to. Others - a small percentage - are from people who appear to be deeply disturbed. But above all they have to be treated with caution because they come predominantly from middle-class viewers who are more used to writing letters to newspapers or indeed writing lengthy statements of any kind. Over and above such sources the professionals of television have the reactions they elicit as members of society mixing with their fellows, the scraps of information they glean from members of the public or from their circle of friends and acquaintances. While it is certainly possible to gather some clues from such sources, no one would seriously claim that, together, they give a very detailed or necessarily a very accurate picture of the audience and its reactions. The fact is that there is no organised way in which members of the audience can communicate with the programme-makers on a continuing basis. There are occasional public meetings, such as those which have been organised by the Independent Broadcasting Authority to discover public reactions to the policies of the Authority and of the local commercial television contractors, which chiefly demonstrate that the representatives of the Authority have a limited view of what constitutes public debate. There are the advisory committees which have been set up by the television organisations to act as contact or pressure groups; but they are heavily weighted towards the professional and middle classes.

Some television producers, faced by the difficulty of knowing anything very precise about their audience, attempt to define that audience for themselves. They will see their viewers as being 'like my Aunt Edith' or as being members of a nuclear family of two parents and two children. They are not always as confident as one television producer who announced at a television conference that he was quite clear about his audience: it stretched from the Queen to the office-cleaner. Of all these pictures of 'the audience' the most accurate is that of the family group. The broadcasters are addressing a small unit of people of different ages in a living-room. Although its members may exchange opinions about the programme later on or next day with the members of other similar groups, the family unit has no link with others except by telephone during transmission. This represents, it can be argued, a true picture of how most people spend an important portion of their lives - their spare time. It is certainly the case that many viewers think of television programmes as something from outside which they allow to penetrate into the family circle. Protests from viewers whose sensibilities, whether moral or political, have been offended by some item on the screen often take the form: 'I do not want such filth in my living-room' or more concretely 'I do not wish to have that person in my living-room'. A good deal of the anger caused by the discussion of sexual morality, by occasional nudity or by 'bad' language, stems from the fact that members of a family may not wish to be forced to react to certain images or words in the presence of others. The embarrassment they feel is transferred to the broadcasting organisation, the director of the programme or the writer of the script.

The view of the audience as predominantly split up into family units is reflected in much of what we see on the screen - from the commercials, in which a housewife guarantees the continuing happiness of her family by buying Brand X corn flakes or using Brand Y lavatory disinfectant, to the current affairs programmes which are addressed explicitly to 'those of you sitting at home'. Social and political questions are presented in terms of the family and of its budget, as if the only interests of the individual members of that family were those defined in terms of home, the fireside and the television set. Occasionally viewers are assumed to have special 'minority' interests which are catered for in gardening programmes, cookery programmes and children's programmes; but the activities discussed are usually home-centred. Yet there are many other ways in which the members of the audience could be defined: as men and women and young people with interests, problems and social aims outside the family circle, as trade unionists, as citizens who spend as much time in their work-places, in trade unions, in political parties, in study groups, in a wide range of activities as in the living-room. It can be argued that by neglecting these other ways of defining the members of the audience television reinforces that process of socialisation in small groups which many forces in our society are happy to perpetuate.

All communicators 'place' their audience, define it as part of a social group or assume that it has certain common aims and interests. The form of words which speakers choose to begin their address at once tells us how they regard us as members of audience, whether it be 'My Lords, Ladies and Gentlemen,' or 'Brothers and Sisters' or 'Comrades'. When Stalin spoke to the Russian people shortly after the German invasion of their country in the summer of 1941 his listeners were at once aware that some important change in the official line had taken place - a change that aimed to rally all sections of the population to fight the Great Patriotic War; they knew because his opening words on the radio were: 'Comrades, brothers and sisters', a form of addresss they had not heard from him before. The business of placing, defining, situating the audience is one that goes on throughout the whole of television. One method is to suggest to the audience what it, as 'the public', thinks or feels about certain topics of public debate and certain situations in which its members may be involved. This is one of the ways in which television can - with varying success - attempt to mould opinion among its audience. Thus, as has been seen during the strikes of 1978-79, the television audience was frequently told that 'the public' was fed up with strikes, that 'the public' would not stand for much more, that 'the public' resented strikers in the public services. Sometimes the concept of 'the public' was extended to include the programme presenters who in interviews would use phrases like 'we, as members of the public'. The presenters, the viewers and 'the public' were thus, it was suggested, part of a body that shared the same thoughts and feelings - although, of course, many of 'the public' were themselves on strike. The identification of audience and presenters is apparent in other ways as in the following typical exchange: Presenter X: 'Well, that is all for just now. Tomorrow we shall be looking at this question again and I hope you will join us.' Presenter Y: 'Thank you, X. I expect we shall'. This method of playing upon the supposed identity of interests between the programme presenters and the audience/public is an important kind of bonding - one of the ways in which the concept of a consensus is established.

Communication of any kind could naturally not take place unless there were some shared views common to the audience and the communicators. What has to be considered in the case of television is the extent to which it contributes towards shaping these views. In comedy shows, for instance, it is assumed that certain situation will be experienced as funny by a large portion of the audience; their views on a wide variety of questions, from the relationships between the sexes to racial relations, are taken for granted and the jokes are made to fit these assumptions. Thus in the comedy series *It Ain't Half Hot, Mum*, set in wartime India, the viewers are expected to find the racist jokes about Indian servants funny - just as they are assumed to be amused by the even more overt racism of *Mind Your Language*, which holds immigrants, black, or otherwise, up to ridicule. In *On the Buses* or *The Rag Trade* workers and trade unions were made the objects of what the programme-makers would describe as good-humoured fun but which, in other terms, could be described as a mockery of trade unions, of the working class and of black workers. In other comedy series the objects of fun are women, presented as being helpless, scheming, manipulative. The audience sitting at home is expected to react with laughter and is encouraged to do so by the sound of studio laughter, by the fact that the shows are introduced as being highly entertaining and by the write-ups in the programme journals. Sometimes the attempt is made to dismiss the view of comedy set out above as being one that takes entertainment shows too seriously; comedy shows are 'only entertainment', their defenders argue, and one must not read too much into them. But a racist joke is no less racist for being funny or even witty. To invite the audience to laugh at the joke is to invite its collusion - its pleasurable collusion - with the views on race encapsulated in the punch-line. It is fair to say that many of the men and women who work in television light entertainment (what, someone once asked, would heavy entertainment be like?) are not themselves racist. It all depends, they will argue, on the context in which the racist joke is made, and might go on to assert that when it is placed in the mouth of a pompous and ridiculous sergeant-major - as is often the case in *It Ain't Half Hot, Mum* -the audience will, while laughing, see the joke as stupid. This was the argument behind the Alf Garnett series in which the chief character was racist, sexist, and reactionary in all his views on society. These views were not shared by either the author of the series or by the chief actor; nor was their aim to encourage the opinions which as they believed, the series held up to ridicule. But the indications are that wherever the series has been shown - in Britain or in the United States or Germany (the last two in local adaptations) - the effects have by no means what the author intended. If racism is widely spread in a society, as it is in ours, such shows will be seen by a considerable part of the audience as validating their views. Comedy - whether in the form of a verbal joke or in the form of a situation comedy - is of great importance. To criticise the use made of it is not to deny its place in human communication or to overlook the fact that comedy is probably always unfair. Would the bureaucrats in an eastern bloc society take kindly to a series which attacked their inefficiencies and petty tyrannies? What is crucial is the position which the programme aims to make its audience adopt as it watches and listens.

It goes without saying that the same process is at work in serious television such as television drama. In this field one of the most marked trends has recently been towards nostalgia - for the Edwardian era, for the First World War, for the period between the wars and even for the Second World War. This is a phenomenon of considerable interest and importance which is characterised by the interpretation of history in terms of personal and usually romantic relationships and of aesthetics; which is the essence of costume drama as presented on television. (The ultimate extension of the genre is represented by the exhibition at Hampton Court, i.e. in a Tudor setting, of the costumes designed for the BBC series on the Tudor monarchy.) The audience in this case is invited to consider history as a process in which the motive forces are not class relations but affairs of the heart, whether the protagonists be the Duke and Duchess of Windsor or fictional characters like the Forsytes. It is a view of history which considers the productive relationships and class struggle to be marginal phenomena. It is a comforting view to put about on the mass media in a time of political and economic crisis. How such trends come about is difficult to explain. It is wrong to see them as the outcome of some extensive and conscious conspiracy. Rather it is the case that the programme-makers are members of a class that feels deep insecurity and are reaching back to those periods of recent history in which the values which they cherish were apparently secure. In this context even the experiences of a young nurse in the gore of the hospitals during the First World War - as portrayed in the adaptations of Vera Brittain's *Testament of Youth* - can be aestheticised and made not only suitable for viewing by a family audience but also made to seem a positive experience of life. The trend towards nostalgia is not confined to television programming but is part of a diffused cultural process which finds expression in fashion trends, in advertising, in the photographs in the colour supplements and in the *bric-à-brac* for sale in the smart antique shops. The men and women who work in television are keenly aware of shifts in fashion, whether they concern the clothes we wear or the ways we are expected to look at history. Although it is difficult to pin such shifts precisely to concrete economic facts - such as the state of sterling or the rate of inflation or the condition of industry at a particular point in time - it is, however, obvious that the insecurity to which we have drawn attention above is a reflection of the general, deep economic crisis of capitalism and of the political crises which accompany it. The importance of the media people is that they transmit their own reactions to these crises to a mass audience and invite that audience to share their reactions - including the escapism which is inherent in a romantic return to the past. To accept their reading of history is to accept a specific way of looking at society and human relationships within it. In this case too we may speak of 'preferred readings' which are reinforced by the authority of the broadcasting institutions that produce them with persuasiveness and professional skill.

3 The Programme-Makers

Who are the programme-makers? What is their background? How do they know what is permissible and what is not?

They are by social origin predominantly but not exclusively middle class. If they have their origins in the working class they will in all probability have been assimilated into the middle class in the course of their education which will normally include not only full-time education up to the age of seventeen or eighteen but further education at college, polytechnic or university. At one time there was a predominance of bright young men - the so-called 'high flyers' - from Oxford and Cambridge among those recruits to the BBC who were thought of as potential senior executives or even as Director Generals; today the net is cast wider, but since the opportunities in our society for higher education are restricted, broadcasters are recruited from a restricted social sample which includes only a small proportion of women. The process of selection is at its most formal in the BBC, which at an early stage adopted a appointment procedure similar to that of the Civil Service - indeed at one time BBC appointment boards included a representative of the Civil Service Commissioners, whose function was to see that roughly the same 'standards' as those of the Civil Service were maintained: that is to say, that the same type of person was recruited with the same educational background and the same class and social outlook. (His main way of establishing the candidate's *bona fides* was to ask detailed questions about the public school the candidate had attended, about what games he had played and what the name of his house-master had been.) Interview by an appointment board is preceded by a preliminary screening process whereby the appointments department eliminates all those who on paper do not seem to have the requisite educational qualifications, the proper background and the necessary references. As for the appointments board itself, it is a test of the candidates' self-confidence, of their ability to verbalise, to 'field' awkward questions - the cricketing metaphor is typical and significant - to present themselves well. Appearance before an appointments board is a special type of interrogation which favours certain types of personality and works strongly against others - those who are not verbally agile, whose skills are intuitive or who are unfamiliar with the conventions of discourse employed by the members of the board. In the case of the BBC there was a further criterion which in some cases eliminated candidates who are otherwise seen as being bright and eligible. That criterion is expressed in the question: 'Will they make good BBC material?' - that is to say, do they give indications of being prepared to undergo the process of institutionalisation, of moulding into a 'BBC man or woman', who will understand what is required of them at all points in their careers. It is a criterion which has been known to exclude candidates who were otherwise eminently suitable but who were suspected of being mavericks and not 'organisation men'. Such signs of being impatient of restraints are not necessarily indications of political radicalism whether of the left or the right, but they are not acceptable in an employee in what has been described as 'a corporate citizen of the United Kingdom'.

Once the board has made its choice successful candidates are subjected to a further filtering process - vetting by the security services of the state, which also report on performers employed by the BBC. At this point those who have been politically active on the left can expect to be turned down - as can others who have without political commitment been associated with persons known to be active in this way. Occasionally it happens that the BBC commits itself to someone before vetting has been carried out; when the vetting is negative the BBC then discovers 'organisational reasons' why the appointment can no longer be made. The rejected person then goes on a black list and is unlikely ever to be employed by the

BBC. The investigative reports produced on staff and performers by the security services are testimony to the amount of petty espionage and surveillance to which citizens of our society are subjected and, like much security work, is occasionally ludicrous in its results. There are, however, gradations in the vetting system so that a person may be employed so long as it is not in a 'sensitive area' of programme-making - that is an area which deals with political matters, classified information, knowledge of government intentions or of the BBC's connection with the defence communications system in the case of a national emergency.

The processes of selection in the commercial television companies is slightly different and somewhat less formal. The relationship of the companies to the state are not so formal as those of the BBC, and the show business background of some of the founders of commercial television leads them to rely less on the procedures of the establishment than does the BBC, although there is evidence of close contacts with the security services and the exchange of information with them. What is common to both BBC and the commercial television companies, however, is the process of learning the rules of the institution, which begins as soon as anyone is appointed to their staff. This process is mainly an informal one and is at work in any large organisation. It is true that in the case of the BBC there are in-house training courses, which are a formal part of the process of moulding staff so that they will function well and efficiently within the limits set by the organisation; but as in other organisations much of what the newcomers learn is picked up from colleagues at work, in the canteen or in the pub favoured by their associates. They may learn that a story or programme idea which they consider 'interesting' is not so, that certain people are not suitable subjects for interview, or that certain words to describe persons or events are 'inappropriate', that a particular piece of film is not suitable for inclusion in a programme or only in certain circumstances or in certain contexts. Newcomers are expected to assimilate such lessons quickly. Both at work and at breaks in work they hear discussion of incidents in the newsroom, of crises in the control gallery, of good and bad judgements, and learn which members of the organisation are believed to be in the ascendant or in decline. It is a learning process that continues for as long as the recruits continue to be employed by the organisation. On the basis of such exchanges, both formal and informal, members of staff in great organisations like these learn to interpret changes of policy or to switch loyalties as executives come and go.

To information acquired in the day-to-day contacts of work and leisure must be added the contents of the directives which filter down through large organisations from policy meetings. These are gatherings of senior executives at which gate-keeping in the grand manner goes on, where - in the news departments, for instance - decisions are taken as to which events should be covered by film or television cameras, where it is laid down what names should be applied to groups or individuals and who shall be allowed access to the microphone or television camera. Membership of such policy-making committees is restricted but there are departmental meetings at which the directives emanating from the policy-makers are passed on, discussed and interpreted. By participating at meetings at departmental level newcomers learn how the organisation works, what policies it pursues, what degree of latitude is possible within the bounds of policy. They learn here and by experience in what directions the organisation is prepared to be liberal and what directions it is not. They will become aware over a period of time of changes in policy and discover that within the organisation there are different tendencies, for even an organisation like the BBC is not monolithic; it can accommodate what are seen - in organisational terms - as progressives and conservatives. There are those who wish to alter methods of operation, who advocate change in programming policy or in the way material is presented on the screen; there are those who resist all change. In the post-war BBC, for example, there was a powerful group which opposed the very idea of television news and insisted that television repeat, over still photographs, a recording of the main radio bulletin. There are differences of opinion over how political issues should be handled and what politicians should be asked to participate in programmes; there are disagreements about what is 'interesting' and 'important'. Powerful representatives of different tendencies have their own supporters; newcomers will find that they may be expected to declare themselves for one faction or another. But above all they must learn the limits of the possible - the limits set by the management of the BBC, by the management of the television companies and by their supervisory body, the Independent Broadcasting Authority.

This view of the process of adaptation which takes place within television organisations was challenged by an ex-Director General of the BBC on the grounds that it is 'marxist determinism', which he considered incompatible with democracy because 'democracy assumes a reality of choice'. But Marx never denied the reality of choice and stated categorically that 'Men make their own history'; what he added was that 'they do not make it just as they please', but 'under circumstances directly encountered, given and transmitted from the past'. A sub-editor in the newsroom at BBC Television Centre or in ITN has 'a reality of choice' when writing a story on a strike, on a PLO raid into Israel or on an attack by Israeli bombers on Palestinian refugee camps in Lebanon. That choice includes whether to describe the strike as 'disruptive' or not; whether to call the PLO raiders 'freedom fighters' or not; whether to describe the Israeli attack as 'terrorism' or not. The question is what constraints does the organisation, given its history and its social role, place on the sub-editor's choice of words. In Zimbabwe, as we have seen, the end of UDI and a shift in the balance of power within neo-colonialism meant that broadcast journalists in Salisbury had to learn to apply a new vocabulary to the members of the African guerilla forces - indeed, had to learn that men like Mugabe could be mentioned at all. Sub-editors, programme editors, script-writers and directors working in television must learn to make the correct choices and become able to make them without reflection, as if they were their own judgements. If they are unable to conform to the usually unwritten rules governing such choices they will not find it easy to work inside the organisation; nor will the organisation be anxious to employ them. That too is an example of the 'reality of choice'. They will be told that they do not have 'news sense' - which means the ability to judge the language and attitudes permissible within the opinion-forming organisations of our society. This ability to make the right judgements becomes so much a part of those who possess it that they are convinced that their choices are merely 'commonsense' and therefore unchallengeable judgements about society, economic relations, politics, morals. Such 'commonsense' views about society are ideology. Those who work in television are engaged in the working and re-working of the ideology of capitalist society.

To people outside television the medium appears to offer a glamorous and exciting opportunity for professional involvement and creativity. Undoubtedly there is among the makers of television programmes, among the electronic engineers who make television possible or among the variety of service departments on which production depends, a great deal of creativity.

But the fact is that television is an industry and those who work in it are industrial workers. A television complex like the BBC's Television Centre is an electronic factory in which the production (or manufacture) of television programmes is organised on industrial lines. The same rules apply to its running and management as to the management of an industrial plant of comparable size and complexity. In a studio complex, too, the concepts of productivity, of through-put, of proper and effective use of plant and equipment are constantly in the minds of management; to these, in the case of the commercial television companies, is added the need to be profitable. It follows that, if a television organisation has six studios, management will wish to see that they produce a steady flow of programmes, just as it will wish to see that no production areas are idle. The same management techniques are applied as are used in a car-factory or in a factory producing television sets. The only substantial difference between them and a television complex is that, in the case of television, the end-product is programmes for transmission to viewers (or for sale to other television organisations) and that the raw materials include the ideas and creativity provided by the set designers, camera crews, directors, producers, and all the other groups of workers who contribute to the making of any programme. The other important difference is that the product of a television complex has, generally, a very short life; built-in obsolescence is the essence of television programmes, which are made to be forgotten.

The fact that the production of television programmes is highly industrialised has important effects on the programmes which we see on our screens and on the procedures employed to realise them. Like any other industry, television is based on the division of labour. A director does not work as a member of a camera crew or as a film or video-tape editor; nor does a member of a camera crew or a film-editor have the opportunity to direct programmes, which means that they cannot exercise final control over editorial and artistic decisions and may not even be consulted about them. This high degree of specialisation is formalised inside the television organisations by the division of the work-force into different grades, which form an ascending ladder up which it is theoretically possible to climb into the upper reaches of management. Much of the time, energy and ingenuity of the administrators of a television organisation is spent in perfecting the grading system - a process in the course of which distinctions of theological subtlety are made between one category of worker and another. It is a process in which the unions recognised by the television organisations are also involved, although - since there is no fundamental community of interest between employers and workers - their aims differ from those of the employers. The latter are anxious to maintain distinctions between groups of workers - arguing, for example, that special skills, which might carry with them higher pay, are used only by a small section of a particular group. Such arguments have two aims: to keep down the wages bill and to create differences between workers in order to divide them. The grading system is therefore a control system. The unions, for their part, play the same subtle grading games as the employers but with a different aim. They strive to impose their own interpretation of the grading system, negotiate in order to have as many people as possible included in the better paid categories and take industrial action, if necessary, to force the employers to pay higher wages and to recognise that new techniques require new skills, which have to be rewarded. They argue that it is only by constantly fighting for higher wages for all grades, including the best paid ones, that everyone on the grading ladder has a chance of an adequate standard of living in the face of inflation. This argument cannot be faulted in a capitalist system in which the aim of the employer must constantly be to increase profitability at the expense of the workers; in a socialist society where the attitudes to work and to the division of labour would be different it would have to be re-examined. Within our own society, the concentration on matters of grading and of wages by the television unions has lead to an attitude which maintains that what is sometimes called the 'nitty-gritty' of industrial life is the only aspect of trade-union activity that matters. Thus organised workers in the television industry will argue that the nature of the programmes which they help to make is none of their business; that they are not there to pass judgement on programme output except at a technical level; and that therefore there is no question of their using their power politically by blacking screens, for instance, when programmes are attacking the workers, supporting racism and sexism, or slandering the trade-union movement.

The grading structure, as we have seen, is like a ladder which theoretically anyone can scale - and in commercial television in particular there have been cases of technicians arriving at managerial levels; but there are a number of obstacles in the grading structure which make such rises difficult. It is particularly difficult to move from being a technician to what are called 'creative grades' - those which are directly concerned with aesthetic and policy decisions. In most television organisations it is fairly common to meet men or women who have accepted employment at a technician's grade only to find that the barriers against passing from one category to another are very hard to overcome. The rigid hierarchies of industrialisation not only lead to frustration and disillusionment in their victims; they also mean that people who could contribute creatively to programme-making are cut off from the opportunity to do so. A further consequence of industrialisation, which treats people as 'bodies' to be fitted onto a work roster, is that they are not involved in the planning of their work and have as little real influence on the end product as they would have on an assembly line. Film crews, for instance, will find themselves scheduled to shoot material for a programme about which they know little and about which they have not been consulted. The result is that they often have scant interest in what they produce. They will turn up on the right day at the right time and carry out their work 'professionally' - which means that they will bring to bear on the task in hand a number of known and tried skills that will produce predictable results. The exposure time will be correct and the picture sharp; the subject will be shot in such a way that the pictures can be edited together into a coherent narrative; the sound will be clear and capable of being easily synchronised with the pictures. They may then move on, on the same day, to another assignment for a different programme about which they are also ill-informed but which they will shoot with the same professional skill. Apart from checking on the technical quality of their work, the team will show little interest in how their pictures are used and have no say in that use. The result is a state of alienation - a situation in which the worker is divorced from the products of his or her own skills. They are, as Marx said, 'related to the product of their labour as to an alien object'. This state of alienation explains the cynicism with which technical crews discuss their assignments or comment on the actual progress of the shooting. Their sharp and often well-directed comments on the behaviour and ideas of the 'creative' members of the production team, or on the subjects being filmed or video-taped, are their weapons against a feeling that they are not properly valued as human beings with special skills. They are placed in this alienated position because it would, in management terms, be uneconomical for a film crew to be involved in the discussion of programme ideas of how the programme should be shot. Time spent in this way would, from management's point of view, be 'wasted' time - time in which the crew might have been producing more material, shooting more film, and so justifying the cost of their wages. It is only rarely - and then only because the director has a reputation - that a television organisation is persuaded to allow a camera crew or a film editor to be involved in the planning and shaping of a programme in a way that not only combats alienation but demands from each crew member positive engagement in the production of the programme.

Within a large television organisation studio, crews, designers, film editors and directors, are frequently allocated to programmes in an impersonal and arbitrary manner. The fact that much of the planning of production schedules is now computerised has accentuated the trend towards impersonal allocation of resources and personnel. One of the effects is, as we have seen, that there is a divorce between the individuals who contribute their various skills to the production and the end-product which appears on our screens. It is a method of working which has effects that extend beyond those on the men and women involved; it also sets its mark on the product of their work - the television programmes themselves. To understand why this should be so we have to return to the concept of television as an industry like any other. If a management group is concerned with productivity it will be best pleased if it can make long-range projections about the use of the labour force at its disposal and of its resources, which in the case of television are the studios, editing suites, camera crews, set-designers, carpenters, electricians, directors and their immediate assistants. They will also prefer to be able to plan a series of products which do not vary greatly in their demands on either resources or labour, which require, that is to say, much the same amount of time and labour on set-building, the same number of make-up artists, costume designers and so on. What is to be avoided at all costs is over- or under-use of resources; what is aimed at is called 'a regular strike', which is nothing to do with the withdrawal of labour but is a production rhythm which can be calculated and repeated with ease. Unfortunately such rationalised planning, which is highly effective when the end-product is uniform and identical, as in a car factory, makes it difficult to accommodate a television programme which is exceptional either in the time it takes to produce, the amount of labour it involves, the number of film or electronic camera crews it requires, or the time it takes to edit the film or tape. Industrial planning pushes television towards programme series which require much the same amount of effort at all levels - hence the increasing trend towards series in the schedules of the BBC and the commercial television companies. An evening's viewing soon demonstrates that the output has been homogenised. The 'regular strike' does not like programmes which make what are seen as exorbitant demands on resources or require longer to produce than normal; nor does it encourage experiment or thought about the use of the medium. In commercial television innovations are particularly difficult to introduce because there is no guarantee that they will draw the same audience and therefore have the same ratings as what they have displaced; which is one of the reasons for the extraordinarily long life of a programme like *Coronation Street*. The result is that programmes tend to fall into well-defined categories, to be made according to formulae which will 'work', and to be turned out very professionally using a limited number of well-tried production techniques. These techniques, which are certainly effective, especially when a director and team are working under the pressure of time (in television as elsewhere in industry time is money) are rarely questioned, although it is clear that there are other and equally effective ways of presenting pictures on a television screen. Instead they have been accepted as 'the grammar of television'. Variations - departures from the traditional grammar - it is argued will simply confuse the audience. If the product is acceptable to the audience why alter anything? Why disturb the smooth flow of the production line?

Like most industrial processes, the production of television programmes takes place in organisations which are highly centralised. Decision-making takes place at the highest levels of the organisation and is the work of a restricted group of senior management, which only exceptionally includes any women. The shaping of the organisation into a pyramid of power helps to achieve the aim of close control not only of finance, production, capital investment and resources but of policy. The process of increased control can be traced in both the BBC and the commercial television companies but, as so often, the BBC presents the clearest example. In its case the development of industrial organisation can be seen to have taken an important step forward in the 1960s when there was a large expansion of both staff and resources in order to set up the second channel: BBC2. Up to this point the organisation of BBC television had, in the view of the organisation and management experts, been rather 'untidy'. The various production departments - drama, entertainment, currents affairs and documentaries, sport and outside broadcasts - had enjoyed a considerable degree of autonomy. At the regular departmental meetings the programme-makers could participate in discussion of both past programmes and future plans and thereby have some say in what appeared on the screen. They also felt that they were able, to some degree, to influence BBC programme policy. They were part of a production team with a specific contribution to make to what was included in the programme schedules. The introduction of BBC2 and its attendant expansion of staff and facilities led to organisational changes devised by O and M (the organisation and management teams), who proposed the splitting of what were now admittedly numerically large departments into smaller sections, each with its appropriate bureaucracy. This development meant a significant growth of 'middle management' - of non-productive officials who interposed their authority between the programme-makers and their heads of department; as a result the 'creative' staff felt that their ability to influence programme decisions had been considerably reduced. They were no longer 'creative' workers who carried out projects of their invention and choice but specialists allocated to tasks in which they might have little or no involvement. This, as we have seen, had long been the normal condition under which television technicians worked; it was a new experience for programme-makers. They were therefore faced by a contradiction between the way they regarded themselves - as individuals with a distinctive contribution to make to a creative process - and the role assigned to them in an industrial process. Realisation of the change in their status and role led to widespread discontent among directors and producers, who were vocally critical of BBC management on the grounds that they were being used like workers on a production line, applying their skills to material in which they often felt little real interest. They also felt that too much power was being delegated to administrators who were not themselves 'creative' and did not therefore understand the problems of the men and women who had to invest their energies and ingenuity in the process of making programmes. This discontent was one of the main causes of what was mistakenly taken to be a radical movement within television organisations in Britain. It is true that some individuals were radicalised by their experiences in the sixties and early seventies and by membership of organisations which aimed to reform both BBC and ITV; but the majority were neutralised by the institutions to which they belonged. They were radicals in an institutional and not a political framework. What the discontent of those days did throw up was the important question, which is still debated today, namely whether it is possible to change the great broadcasting institutions from within or whether they can only be changed by a change in society. It is a question to which we shall return. It confronts those who work in the television companies for they not only produce programmes, they also perpetuate a view of society which reinforces and sustains the present social order. Television is one of the important agencies which help to reproduce our society, to support and protect it from radical change and above all from changes in the system of property-ownership on which it is based.

4 The Controllers

In Britain the men and women who are, in law, responsible for what is seen on television are neither the directors, the heads of programmes, the company chairmen of the ITV programme companies nor the Director General of the BBC, but the Governors of the BBC and the Governors of the Independent Broadcasting Authority (originally the Independent Television Authority, whose scope has been extended to include commercial radio) and their respective Chairmen. (It is significant that the former head of the IBA, Lady Plowden, who was in her time Deputy Chairman of the BBC, was referred to as its 'Chairman'.) All of them, including the chairpersons, are men and women drawn from the list of 'the good and the great' kept in Whitehall by the Director of the Public Appointments Unit of the Civil Service Department. This list contains the names of those 4000 citizens who have been recommended to successive governments as trustworthy enough to be called upon to accept duties on official and semi-official bodies, government committees of enquiry, and so on, and of whom only a small percentage are women. It must be said that the Governors of the BBC or of the IBA are not appointed on a party basis; that is to say, a Conservative prime minister will not necessarily appoint a Conservative to a place on either of the Boards of Governors or to be Chairman of the Corporation or the Authority. Thus the Thatcher government appointed a safe ex-Labour peer to be Deputy Chairman of the IBA with a view to his succeeding to the Chairmanship in due course. The fact that political patronage for public office of this kind is not determined by party loyalties is sometimes pointed to as one of the virtues of the British broadcasting system. That system, we are encouraged to believe, has the concept of neutrality and balance enshrined in its governing bodies. An analysis of the kind of people who have been appointed to the two Boards gives a rather different picture.

When the British Broadcasting Corporation came into being in January 1927, it replaced the British Broadcasting Company, a consortium of radio manufacturers, who had joined together to broadcast programmes (so that people would have an incentive to buy wireless sets) and to persuade the government of the day to protect them from 'unfair competition' from manufacturers in the United States, Germany and Austria. It carried over from its previous existence as a business cartel its General Manager, John Reith, who thus became the first Director General of the Corporation which by its existence relieved the manufacturers of the need to pay for putting on programmes and left them free to enjoy the rapidly expanding market for sets. The Corporation did, however, acquire a new board of directors. The chairman was the Earl of Clarendon, who had been Conservative chief whip in the House of Lords; he was joined by Lord Gainham, a coal owner (the coal owners had starved the striking miners back to work in the autumn of 1926), Sir Gordon Nairne, formerly Comptroller of the Bank of England, and Dr Montague Rendall, an ex-head of Winchester public school. He, in a typical piece of establishment patronage, was recommended for the post by the Postmaster General who had been his pupil at Winchester. The government of the day, which was Baldwin's Conservative ministry and which had just emerged victorious from the General Strike - Reith was knighted for his services during that strike - felt that this list had to be supplemented by a Labour figure and chose Mrs Snowden, wife of the first Labour Chancellor of the Exchequer and the man who in the National Government of 1931 cut the unemployment benefit.

With this first Board the pattern was set. Other appointments have included a former First Lord of the Admiralty, who had also been Home Secretary and President of the MCC, the old-Etonian brother of the Governor of the Bank of England; the President of the Scottish Accountants in London; a former Inspector General of the Royal Ulster Constabulary (to represent the audience in Northern Ireland); Lord Tedder, responsible for saturation bombing in Germany; an ex-headmaster of Rugby College; an ex-Ambassador who occupied what is known significantly as 'the Foreign Office seat' on the Board; an ex-head of the Foreign Office; and the chairman of Rio Tinto, with its extensive holdings in what was still Franco's Spain. Neither the inclusion of a few right-wing Labour figures like Barbara Wootton nor of the black cricketer, Learie Constantine, who saw nothing wrong in *The Black and White Minstrels*, has had much effect on the solid representation of the interests of the British ruling class in broadcasting over the last fifty years. A recent study of how the BBC is governed gives an interesting breakdown of the governors' backgrounds and careers from which it emerges that 21 out of 85 were drawn chiefly from finance or business, while six had trade union backgrounds. Thirteen had spent most of their lives in some branch of the social services; eleven had held high office in the diplomatic service or the Foreign Office. 'Sixteen had shown considerable interest in the arts.' The men and women called upon to take office in the Independent Television Authority, when commercial television was set up in 1955, were no different in class background or in class interests.

Clearly, to suggest that such men and women represent in any way the views and interests of the bulk of British viewers would be ridiculous. What they do represent are the ideas and values shared by some of the most important groups within the British ruling class, of ideas which are also those of the parliamentary consensus - that body of opinion which unites the Conservative, Labour and Liberal parties in their Westminster club. It is clear that a governing body with such a membership and such ideas on society, on taste and on public morality (including censorship) is unlikely to guide either the BBC or the ITV companies along radical lines or to encourage programmes which might in any real way endanger the present social system. Even what in the light of history appear comparatively harmless ideas have been blocked by them. Thus, before the Second World War, the Chairman of the BBC, under pressure from the Foreign Office, banned a pacifist talk by a former German submarine commander. In 1933 the Board of Governors banned

Vernon Bartlett, a liberal journalist, from the microphone because of a broadcast remark that displeased Prime Minister MacDonald. In 1935 they connived with the government to postpone and finally lose a series of talks called *The Citizen and His Government*, which was to have included contributions by Harry Pollitt of the Communist Party of Great Britain and by Oswald Mosley of the Blackshirts. (It must in fairness be added that the Foreign Office was as opposed to Mosley as to Pollitt.) During the Second World War the Board refused to allow Lord Beveridge to broadcast on the Beveridge Plan, which was the basis of the liberal reforms that led to the setting up of the welfare state, arguing that it would only do so if the government approved the script. This the government declined to do on the grounds, apparently, that discussion of social changes in the post-war period might distract people from the war effort or, as the Conservative MP for Cambridge University put it in a Commons debate, because people might think that 'we are more interested in social reform than in questions of strategy and frontiers'. The Governors of the IBA, for their part, have shown their awareness of what is called the national interest by banning a Granada Television programme, *South of the Border*, a view of affairs in Ulster as seen from Dublin, even before filming had been completed. There are a number of similar cases on both sides.

It would, however, be a gross simplification to believe that the governing bodies of the BBC and the IBA are simply putty in the hands of government. While their individual and corporate judgements are determined by their idea of the public good and the basic interests of the British ruling class (which they equate), they do from time to time have differences of opinion with government over their relationship to the central power of the state and over the degree of direct pressure which government can openly apply to them. Thus, to go back to the case of the German submarine commander, we find that the Chairman of the BBC, who had obediently gone along to Prime Minister Baldwin's office in Downing Street to be told to cancel the talk, then wrote to the Cabinet complaining at 'the impugnment of the Corporation's considered judgement' and going on to state that 'the real issue is a constitutional one'. He points out that 'in the early stages of its existence, one of the greatest obstacles to overcome was the impression that the Broadcasting Company had become a government department' when it became the British Broadcasting Corporation. He agrees that the licence to broadcast granted to the BBC by the Postmaster General gives that minister 'plenary powers' to 'require the Corporation to refrain from sending any matters of any class specified' but argues that a guarantee had been given that this power (which is a blanket power to censor programmes) would not be used except in time of national emergency. In other words, there was a gentlemen's agreement between government and the BBC and government had broken that agreement.

Although in this particular case the BBC yielded to Baldwin's pressure there have been other occasions when the BBC Governors have demonstrated their unwillingness to be pushed into certain courses of action and to cancel programmes because of government pressure. One celebrated instance occurred during the Suez crisis of 1956 when the Eden government was so outraged by the fact that the BBC in its overseas broadcasts did not conceal the deep division in the country over the Suez invasion that there is reason to believe it was prepared to commandeer the BBC. A second case was that of the discussion programme *The Question of Ulster* when the Governors came under strong pressure from the Home Secretary, Maudling, who was the Minister responsible for Northern Ireland, to cancel the programme. In both cases the Governors determined to withstand the pressures - in the case of Suez presumably because they were aware of the degree of support they could expect in parliament and in the press for their stand and, in the case of Ulster, because they knew they could rely on the professional tact of the television officials involved to contain the discussion of *The Question* within very strict limits. The fact has to be recognised that while the Governors of the BBC or the IBA are unlikely to do anything that might be construed as being 'contrary to the public interest' and might - as Wedgewood Benn pointed out when he was Postmaster General - be dismissed if they did so, they are also committed to the concept that the BBC is an organisation that, constitutionally, is independent of government. One could add that it would fail to be as effective as what has been described as an 'ideological state apparatus' if it were not seen, in all but exceptional circumstances to act independently of the central power. The Governors are, for the most part, men and women who have, in their various spheres, been used to the exercise of authority and power; on a purely human level they are likely to resist and resent any attempt to coerce them, particularly if that attempt becomes public knowledge. Nor, within bourgeois democracy as it is practised in

Britain, would the minister responsible be happy to have the BBC or the IBA make a public announcement on air to the effect that a scheduled programme had been cancelled on the instructions of the minister responsible for broadcasting, who is now the Home Secretary.

In this respect the British broadcasting system differs greatly from most other European broadcasting systems. In France, for instance, the control exercised by government over the French radio and television organisation, ORTF, since the end of the Second World War has been open and complete. It was a French socialist minister who described French television news as 'the newspaper of the nation'. During the Algerian war the censorship of newscasts entailed a preview by government and ORTF officials of a pre-recorded bulletin. In Italy, RAI, the state financed company, which for many years enjoyed the broadcasting monopoly, was openly controlled by the Christian Democrat Party, which nominated the Director General and had its men in all the positions of power within the organisation. Political opponents of the christian democrats were for many years simply ignored by television and not only not given access to the cameras in the studios but also not shown in news items. Now the 'historical compromise' has brought about changes which mean that there are communists and socialists high up in the organisation and that the production departments have become centres of power in the hands of christian democrats, communists or socialists. In Germany, political forces are directly reflected in the composition of the governing bodies of the federal broadcasting system in which the political parties, the trade unions, the employers, the churches, youth organisations and many other bodies are represented and act in the interests of their constituencies. These varying patterns of control are the result of the political history of the countries concerned and of the balance of political power within them. In Britain we have a long tradition of sophisticated control of public institutions which stems in part from the compromises reached between social classes - between landowners and industrialists, between industrialists and the trade-union movement - and in part from the experience of an old and very practised ruling class, which is well aware of the seductive appeal of the concept 'public service' and of the ways in which critics can, by incorporation in governing bodies, become the supporters of the 'national interest'. The resulting mechanisms are at once very delicate, in that they react quickly and sensitively to change and crisis, and very robust, in that they adapt easily to changing circumstances. There is certainly a sense in which the BBC and the IBA are independent bodies; it is also true that the men and women who, in law, are these organisations, that is to say the Governors, are perfectly aware of the task they have to perform in society. They are also aware of the sanctions, none the less real for being so far unused, of open censorship and dismissal, which could be used against them. The key to the smooth working of the system is that everyone understands everyone else all ways round.

How the system works was demonstrated very clearly in the crucial year of 1926. In March of that year a committee of enquiry proposed that the British Broadcasting Company should become a corporation under Royal Charter. In May, before the Baldwin government had announced whether or not it had accepted the terms of the committee's recommendations, came the General Strike. There was at once strong pressure from Churchill, the Home Secretary of the day, to take over the BBC as a government radio station in the same way as he had commandeered printing presses in Fleet Street to produce the government propaganda paper, *The British Gazette*. Prime Minister Baldwin was more cautious. The Cabinet was divided. Eventually a Cabinet committee, which Reith was allowed to attend, recommended that broadcasting be left in the hands of the BBC 'to do what was best'. Reith thus found himself in a difficult position for it meant that Baldwin could make him responsible for unpleasant editorial decisions, such as the refusal to allow the Archbishop of Canterbury to broadcast an ecumenical message producing a truce in the strike or to permit Ramsay MacDonald, the Labour leader, to broadcast even if MacDonald was prepared to let Reith edit his text. Meantime BBC news was almost entirely dependent on government sources for news material. Reflecting on the strike in his private diary, Reith recorded his views on why Baldwin and his government had not taken over the BBC. 'They want to be able to say' he wrote, 'that they did not commandeer us, but they know that they can trust us not to be really impartial.' It is a perceptive and important formulation, which is both very accurate and very honest. Such honesty is rare when the role of the media in society is being discussed, partly because it is in the nature of ideology, which is what the media purvey, to conceal such awkward social truths. In a memorandum to his senior staff after the strike, Reith was less frank and attempted a rationalisation of the BBC's role. To them he rested his justification of the BBC's 'impartiality' on the tenuous grounds that the strike was illegal and went on to argue that the BBC, as a national institution, 'was for the government in this crisis' because 'the government in this crisis was acting for the people'. This was one of the earliest, if not the earliest, occasion on which the BBC made the distinction between 'the people' - what today is called 'the public' - and the strikers, as if, by going on strike, the organised working class of Great Britain has ceased to be part of 'the people' and had been rejected by society. It is one of the ironies of broadcasting history that, within the BBC, the General Strike is commonly referred to as the moment when the true independence of the Corporation was demonstrated. What is certain is that in July 1926 parliament agreed to the change in the BBC's status. Reith was knighted in the January Honours list of 1927.

What we do not know - it would be a suitable subject for research if the veil of official secrecy could be penetrated - is how the BBC and the IBA would be expected to act in a state of emergency today. There is every reason to believe that the BBC is firmly integrated into the organisation whereby the country is divided up under regional seats of government under the Regional Commissioners. No doubt there are secure facilities for broadcasting on both radio and television in their underground headquarters. No doubt the main news source would be, as in the case of the General Strike, government hand-outs. No doubt the BBC and the commercial companies of the IBA would collaborate closely with the police, the military and the Regional Commissioners. Independence is a luxury which can readily be jettisoned 'in the national interest'. Neither the BBC nor the IBA is likely to resist.

One of the arguments in favour of the 'non-political' status of the Governors of the BBC or the IBA is that, because they do not, as it were, have any constituency to which they must report back, they are therefore not subject to organised pressures from identifiable forces within society. What exact pressures they are subject to is difficult to determine because their exact interests and connections are not spelt out. But they are people who move freely in the upper reaches of our society; they have frequently been members of the civil service or have dealt with government departments at a high level; they come from the schools and universities from which our politicians, our administrators, judges, clergymen and service officers are still predominantly drawn; they belong to the same clubs as prominent businessmen, civil servants, retired colonial administrators. It is not difficult to imagine the kind of opinions they hear and share, the kind of comments they are likely to hear passed on programmes, on the political situation, on the role of television, on youth, on the feminist movement or on the activities of the left. We shall see later that they have on occasion reported the reactions of ministers to particular programmes, such as the satirical programme *That Was The Week That Was*. If their function is seen as being antennae which transmit the opinions of the public and thus help the corporate body of the BBC - the Board of Governors - to determine policy, then they are highly unrepresentative of the bulk of the population even if they are well-informed on the views of the establishment. The intelligence they gather from their various contacts permits them to make 'correct' decisions - decisions, which do not run counter to the views and requirements of the centres of power in our society. In this sense they perform an important function and can ensure that the BBC and the IBA discharge their task in society effectively as supporters of the established order, as organisations which form the viewers' ideas about society and reproduce its values.

While it is clear that the Governors of an institution like the BBC have an important part to play in shaping the broad policy within which it operates, the day-to-day responsibility rests with the chief executive whom they appoint. He is the Director General, who is also editor-in-chief. The limits within which he operates are not normally defined either by the Board or by the minister responsible for broadcasting although, in the past, the latter has laid certain restrictions on the Corporation. Thus when the Corporation was first set up in 1927 the Postmaster-General instructed it that it was not to broadcast its own opinions on public policy, nor was it to broadcast on matters of political, industrial, or religious controversy. This ban continued for two years when it was withdrawn 'experimentally' and the decision as to what should or should not be broadcast was left to the Governors and their chief executive. In the years after the Second World War the BBC entered into an understanding with the then Labour government, which, typically, was not consigned to paper on the grounds - as expressed by a Labour minister - that 'it is as impossible to formulate exhaustive principles on paper as it is, for instance, impossible to define what conduct is unbefitting an officer and a gentleman'. However that may be, the understanding contained a self-denying ordinance on the part of the BBC which forbade the discussion of a subject about to be debated in parliament within fourteen days of that debate. In 1953 the Board of Governors decided that the rule was unnecessarily restrictive and should be withdrawn unless the main parties objected. This the parties did, supporting the Conservative Postmaster General, Hill (later Chairman in turn of both ITA and BBC) when he issued a regulation formally forbidding the BBC to discuss any issues about to be debated in either house of parliament for a fortnight before the debates. The regulation was not withdrawn until 1956. Today the IBA is required by law not to broadcast anything 'which offends against good taste and decency or is likely to encourage or incite to crime or to lead to disorder or to be offensive to public feeling'. It is a requirement not explicitly laid upon the BBC in its Charter or Licence but agreed to be its duty by the Chairman of the Board of Governors in 1964, thus bringing the BBC into line with the commercial television companies.

Such rules (imposed or self-imposed) apart, the BBC in particular has not normally attempted to give formal definitions of what is or is not permitted on the screen. There is, however, a BBC code governing the representation of violence and a similar code drawn up by the IBA, although there is considerable doubt among media researchers whether violence on the television screen is indeed a cause of violence in real life; its roots are more likely to lie in alienation, in social disintegration and in the effects of repression and brutalisation by social conditions. In general the limits of what is permitted emerge pragmatically, on the basis of decisions about specific programmes. What may be expressed on the screen is determined by the concept of 'the politics of the consensus' - the mainstream of political thinking within our bourgeois democracy. Political ideas that lie outside the mainstream may be discussed but will at the same time be distanced. (Thus a BBC series examining marxism included no marxist speaker.) Consensus politics covers what the television authorities would define as the centre of the political spectrum - a band of opinion which may, from time to time, shift slightly to left or right, and which may expand or contract according to the political climate at any time. Thus, in the period covering the end of the fifties and the beginning of the sixties, which was the period of the post-Korean War boom, there was a noticeable relaxation of restrictions on what could be shown on BBC television, in the choice of topics and the way in which they were treated. This was the period when the Tory Prime Minister Macmillan, announced that we had 'never had it so good'. It was a time in television when playwrights like David Mercer and John MacGrath wrote for television and directors like Tony Garnet and Ken Loach began to establish their reputations as critical commentators on social questions. It was the time, too, of the 'satirical' programmes in which some of the sacred cows of the establishment - the monarchy, the church, leading politicians and other previously taboo targets - were attacked. The Governors of the BBC were from the start nervous about such developments, deprecated what they saw as lapses in taste and began to report from their contacts that some government ministers were inclined to be sensitive; satirical programmes, they indicated, were 'wearing thin'. Such reports and the threatened resignation of one Governor caused *That Was The Week That Was* to be taken off the air; the explanation given for its demise was the purely spurious one that, since there was a general election in the near future, it would have been wrong to continue with a programme of this kind. The commercial companies were noticeably timorous during this period and made no attempt to cash in on the manifest success of 'satirical' programmes; they took refuge behind the Television Act and its references to good taste and decency.

That a satirical programme like *That Was The Week That Was* was ever put on can only be explained in the light of the political and economic conditions of the time. The Conservative government was buoyant; the boom meant that the sales of television sets were rising sharply, which in turn meant that the number of television licences - and therefore the size of the BBC's annual income - was increasing steadily. Because of its sound financial position, which had every sign of continuing for some years, the BBC did not have to face the need to approach government to ask for an increase in the licence fee. Today, when the political and economic situation is vastly different neither Tory or Labour politicians would be likely to tolerate the kind of mockery that was directed at them in the early sixties. Nor is the BBC sufficiently secure financially to take the risk. It is important to remember, in this connection, that the writers and performers in the satirical programmes, who have been very accurately compared to medieval court jesters, were not at all inspired by left-wing views or sympathies; indeed they mostly shared a public school background and represented what can best be described as a right-wing radical tendency more common on the continent than in Britain. It is significant that several of them went on to collaborate on *Private Eye*, which for all its jibes at authority is a deeply reactionary journal, given to anti-semitism and literary 'queer-bashing'.

If, in this period of the BBC's history, the spectrum of opinion was pushed to the left and expanded, it was due to the influence and experience of the Director General of the day, Hugh Carleton Greene, who judged the political situation and concluded that if the BBC were more adventurous it would have the support of large sections of the viewing public and of certain journalists and politicians. His own view of the function of broadcasting was undoubtedly coloured by his experiences in the thirties as a correspondent in nazi Germany, from which he was expelled. They led him to favour political cabaret, which had flourished in pre-nazi Germany - hence the satirical programmes - and to oppose racism. He intimated, for instance, that it was not the business of the BBC to give fascists or racists the opportunity to expound their views because, in his opinion, such views were outside the range of ideas that could be tolerated in a democracy. On similar grounds he excluded communists, a decision which reflected his experience as a chief executive in the BBC's External Services during the height of the Cold War and his activity in counter-insurgency propaganda towards the end of British colonial rule in Malaya. Since his day there has been another shift in the spectrum - this time to the right - and the band-width of what can be shown on television has narrowed. The BBC's financial situation is insecure and it is too vulnerable to government pressures for it to contemplate mounting satirical programmes. Its policy must be not to upset parliament or any other important pressure group.

In making his judgement as to what is possible, an official like the Director General of the BBC requires good sources of intelligence within the establishment. The Governors supply some of that information; the rest he gleans from his own contacts in the press, in parliament, in the civil service, in business and the law. He will make it his business to meet politicians, including cabinet ministers and members of the opposition front bench unofficially - that is to say, socially - by inviting them to dinner at the BBC Television Centre or at Broadcasting House. This gives him an opportunity to sound them out, to discover their views on broadcasting, on future political developments, on foreign policy. He may discuss with them his own projects or discuss the BBC's financial situation, testing their reaction to his statements, canvassing their support. All this highly important exchange of information and opinions is unofficial and off the record, which does not mean that bargains may not be struck and kept.

Other members of the organisation carry out the same intelligence-gathering process at their different levels and in their different areas. A famous head of BBC current affairs programmes, notable among other things for being a woman, has described in her memoirs how the process works. It was during informal discussion with politicians and other important public figures, when they relaxed over a drink after a programme like *Panorama* had gone on the air, that some of the most important exchanges took place. Here reactions to programmes were collected and criticism noted. It was this executive's practice to report the next day in a memorandum to the Director General what she considered to be the most important remarks made by these public figures. They might concern the number of left-wing members of the Labour Party who had been on the air in the previous period, or some other aspect of the balance of power within one of the main parties which was causing anxiety among its leaders and managers. They might be criticisms of news coverage of some item, or of breaches of 'taste'. Memoranda such as she wrote, reports of conversations with prominent establishment figures, are an important part of the intelligence on which the Director General of the day bases political and editorial decisions. For the carrying out of these decisions, however, he must rely on the heads of department and on their staffs. Because of the way in which they are selected they are likely to accept as 'obvious' or 'merely commonsense' the central assumptions of consensual politics in this country - will believe that parliamentary democracy as we know it in Britain has only minor blemishes; will not question the capitalist system; will believe, at best, that a mild form of·social democracy is the answer to the general crisis of capitalism; will respect the monarchy and the other institutions of the British; will, although themselves probably agnostics, believe that it is important to purvey on television the values of 'mainstream christianity', which is the theological equivalent of the political consensus. They do not see themselves as reactionary and indeed will uphold liberal views on a variety of topics like race, feminism, education, the welfare state; a graph of how political attitudes are distributed among them would probably be skewed slightly left of centre. They are unlikely, however - given the nature of the security screening (although a few odd cases have slipped through the net) - to include more than a handful of people who accept the marxist analysis of capitalism or the need to replace it by a socialist society. It is however, one of their professional duties to learn the limits of what is politically possible on television. If they are in any doubt they will refer the matter up to their immediate superior, who - if in doubt - will refer it to his superior and so on. It is a process which can end with the problem being discussed and ruled on by the Board of Governors.

While there are cases where such referral will be justified in institutional terms, members of the BBC's staff are encouraged to make their own decisions - to be their own censors and self-censors, if necessary. There are strong institutional pressures which, by encouraging decisions at lower levels, ensure that the innocuous will be preferred to anything - a phrase, a shot, an idea - which might lead to difficulties within a department or within the Corporation. Why, for instance, should producers employ a director or scriptwriter who will only embroil them with the department head? The tendency towards self-censorship is one of the contributory causes of the blandness of much television - not only in the BBC. Those who are insensitive to the limitations imposed by the institution and its reading of what is possible, or who wilfully transgress the limits - as happened in the case of an interviewer who during transmission pressed Wilson too hard on the morality of supporting the United States in Vietnam - are likely to be transferred to less 'sensitive' areas; in his case to an arts programme.

5 From Public Service to Commercial Television

One of the most important concepts in British broadcasting is the idea of public service. Broadcasting frequencies, the argument goes, are scarce - although there are large sections of the spectrum which are designated as 'not available for broadcasting', being taken up by the police, the diplomatic wireless service, the military, fire-services and no doubt other state organisations; from this it follows that access to the frequencies must be controlled and steps taken to ensure that those who do have access employ their privilege in a public-minded manner. Broadcasters are in a specific sense seen as trustees of the public interest. The concept of public service broadcasting has always been central to the policies of the BBC and it was extended to the Authority set up to control commercial television under the terms of the Television Act 1954 and in subsequent re-enactments of that law. It was an attitude towards broadcasting that chimed in with Reith's puritanical view of the nature of public service and his sense of public morality..Even when he was manager of the British Broadcasting Company, a straightforward business cartel, he began to campaign in its favour. His reasons included his strongly held view that the provision of programmes for radio (and later for television) should not be controlled by commercial interests in the pursuit of profit. 'We have done our best,' he said in 1931, 'to found a tradition of public service rather than public exploitation.' In the following year he expanded on the concept, stating in a public lecture that 'to the right kind of man, a dividend motive is unnecessary. More than this, the serving of public interest and the serving of financial interest are not normally fully compatible.' The idea of an independent public corporation also appealed greatly to him because of his general contempt for politicians and indeed for parliament which, in his old age, he referred to as 'the Mother of Corruption'.

Two points have to be made about Reith's devotion to public service. The first is that it had nothing to do with socialism; his instincts were authoritarian and he recorded in his diary his admiration for Hitler's methods - this after hearing of the purge of the Brown Shirts in which Hitler eliminated the old storm-troopers who had become a political liability. The second is that, however strong his views on the subject, Reith could not have acquired the support to put through the idea of a public corporation to control broadcasting unless it had been in the interests of a number of powerful interests, including the politicians he so despised. That he was well aware of the importance of power in society is clear from his diaries in which he wrote that 'the only unfailing powers are force and money' and went on to add that the monopoly of the BBC depended on solid backing for what he called 'the brute force of monopoly'. The fact is that there was general agreement in the middle twenties among the interests, political and commercial, which gave evidence to the government committee on broadcasting, in favour of the public service idea. As a result that committee, as we have seen, recommended the setting up of the British Broadcasting Corporation with Reith as its first Director General. It is perhaps possible to draw a parallel between the concept of this 'independent' corporation and the marxist concept of the function and origin of the state, which is that 'the state arises where, when and to the extent that class antagonisms cannot be objectively reconciled'. Here it was not a question so much of class as of sectional interests within the ruling class which found in the Corporation 'a special public body standing above them' (to vary slightly Lenin's description of the function of the state). The fact is that Tories, Liberals and Labour at this period were all attracted by the idea of public bodies, which it was believed in some way could reconcile divergent interests and stand above them as custodians of the public interest. Bodies like the Central Electricity Board and the London Transport were all manifestations of a trend towards a form of corporatism. It was an idea which found considerable approval at the time and was the concept behind the fascist state as Mussolini envisaged it - a society vertically organised so as to eliminate class interests and class conflicts. One Conservative newspaper saw the BBC as an example of 'socialism, like a kangaroo progressing by leaps and bounds'; but another more accurately described the setting-up of the Corporation as an example of 'conservative socialism'.

That the Conservative Party did not oppose the setting-up

of this 'socialist' organisation can probably be explained by the combination of a number of factors: the highly satisfactory performance of Reith and his organisation during the General Strike; distaste on the part of the landowning interests and the interests of the heavy industries, which Baldwin represented, for the new industrialists of the radio industry; and the tradition of public service - charitable works, public philanthrophy, service as JPs and magistrates, unpaid service on committees of all kinds - which was strong in the Conservative Party and was one of the relics of the ethos of the landowning aristocracy. The devotion to public service among the Tories was to reassert itself, as we shall see, during the violent debate over the introduction of commercial television, when the same forces came into play and split the Tory Party in two. This concept of social duty, of 'public service', can in certain circumstances be at variance with 'the unacceptable face of capitalism', which was, we should remember, a phrase coined by a Conservative politician. These contradictions within the ruling class, together with wider contradictions, it was thought could be reconciled in the sphere of broadcasting at least by the setting-up of a Corporation which was seen not to be under direct political control, but was yet keenly aware of its social tasks which included 'objective' reporting of news and opinion. Such an organisation, it seems to have been recognised on all sides within the consensus, would best further the maintenance of the established order and its social structures.

The Corporation which was set up by Royal Charter in 1927 'in view of the widespread interest which is shown by Our People in the Broadcasting Service and of the great value of the Service as a means of education and entertainment' - in subsequent versions of the Charter, which is renewed at intervals, the word 'information' was added - was from its beginning a metropolitan-based and highly centralised organisation. The Charter was supplemented by a licence from the Postmaster General allowing the Corporation to broadcast using wireless telephony; giving him the power to lay down the hours of broadcasting, and granting him the reserve powers of censorship whereby the Corporation could be required to refrain from broadcasting any specified matter. The very real powers of the minister were revealed at an early stage. When it came to formal acceptance of the terms of the Charter, Reith pushed the Governors, who had already been appointed, to hold out for a better financial deal over the share of the licence fee allotted to the Corporation. When the Governors showed signs of hesitating to accept the terms, the Postmaster General sent for the Chairman and intimated that unless they did sign other Governors would be appointed who would. So much for independence.

The question of the licence fee is an important one. It has long been maintained by the BBC that one of its sources of strength and independence is that it receives its funds directly from the listeners or - as it is now - the viewers in the shape of the fee they pay for the right to operate a television receiver. The courts have ruled that they must pay this fee, even if they never watch a single BBC programme. In the BBC's version of how it is funded the fact that the licence money is collected by the Post Office, which takes a large fee - £25.5 million in 1978 out of a gross revenue of £287 million - for administering the licence system and investigating interference with BBC signals, and that the licence money is then passed on to the BBC by the Home Office, the department responsible for broadcasting, is seen as merely a piece of necessary machinery. But at various times in the history of the BBC, government has retained large portions of the licence revenue, which have simply gone into the Treasury funds. Thus in 1934, of a gross licence revenue of over £3 million, only just over a half was the BBC's effective net share. It is clear, therefore, that the licence revenue is not the BBC's by absolute right - indeed it was not until the 1950s that it received the full revenue; that the Treasury can from time to time make a levy on its revenue; and that the control of the licence fee is in the hands of government. It is true that the licence is not technically government funding - that is to say it is not allocated by a government department - and that therefore no minister is responsible in parliament for how the money is spent. If it were there could be parliamentary questions and debates on how it was spent - debates, that is to say, on programme content and programme policy; which is what happens, from time to time, in Canada where government funds go to finance broadcasting. But this is very different from the picture of a corporation sustained directly by its audience without government mediation or control. When negotiations were taking place before the increase in the licence fee in 1979 there were hints in the press of the kind of pressure that governments can exercise; the BBC, it was suggested, was in difficulties because a television programme had included an interview with members of the Irish armed group which claimed to have killed the Tory MP, Airey Neave. This, it was suggested, was likely to make the negotiations difficult. In the event the BBC did receive an increased licence fee of £34 for colour television but it had asked for £40 as a realistic figure to meets its needs. It was to be kept on short commons in a period of inflation. Moreover, a change in procedures was announced. In future discussions of the licence fee government would base its conclusions on the presentation to the minister responsible of an estimate of the BBC's future requirements. This opening of the BBC's books to government could mark an important change in relationships between the two bodies and opens up further possibilities of control through finance.

Problems over control are endemic in the relationship. There has always been tension between the restrictive powers, direct and indirect, which are available to government and which led one of Reith's successors to describe the BBC as 'a powerful and efficient instrument, which has all the appearance of independence but which ... (government) can control at will' and the desire of certain executives and programme-makers, for professional reasons, to assert the declared independence of the institution and exploit whatever is progressive in the Reith tradition. It has to be said of this strange and contradictory man that he fought strongly for certain liberties - for the right to broadcast news put together in the BBC newsroom and not delivered by the news agencies, for the right to report on public events and to employ BBC staff as reporters and correspondents. These were the kind of tensions which radio had lived under and which television inherited when it arrived in 1936.

Television had been a long time in coming. Although it had been clear since before the First World War that the transmission of pictures by radio was theoretically possible - in 1908 a British scientist, Campbell-Swinton wrote an article in *Nature*, the scientific journal, describing how television would function, and in Russia in the same year Professor Rosing in St. Petersburg demonstrated the practical possibility of television, there was a long delay in realising the prophecies of scientists. The reasons are to be sought in the priority given to the development of wireless, which was of immense importance to the great powers - Britain, Germany and the United States - for communications during the 1914-18 war, both with overseas colonies and with high seas fleets and between combat units. In the post-war years the slowness with which investment was attracted to television can be explained by the fact that the market for radio receivers and radio equipment generally was far from satisfied. In 1925, however - that is to say a full year before the British

Broadcasting Corporation came into existence - a British experimenter, John Logie Baird, registered a company called Television Limited. In 1926 the Post Office took him seriously enough to grant him a licence to carry out experimental transmissions. His achievements were considerable; they included a trans-Atlantic transmission of still images and transmissions to ships at sea as well as experiments in colour and stereoscopy. Unfortunately he clung obstinately to a mechanical scanner (a revolving disc perforated by a spiral system of holes) for originating his pictures. This system provided low definition pictures of only 30 lines as opposed to what would be the eventual broadcast standard of 405 lines - that being the number of times an electronic beam scanned the display tune of a receiver in 1/50th of a second. (The modern standard is 625 lines). He was also unable to secure the very large funds he would have required to develop his ideas - funds which might have enabled him to realise more quickly that mechanical scanning was not the way forward. His obstinacy in this respect, which eventually came very close to paranoia, was fostered by the attitude of the bureaucrats at the BBC who were in contact with him in 1927-28 and eventually co-operated in carrying out experimental transmission up to 1934.

1934 was an important year for television in Britain. It saw the coming together of a British firm, Electrical and Musical Industries (EMI), which had links with the powerful Radio Corporation of America (RCA) and the British Marconi Company. The board of directors included Marconi himself and David Sarnoff, the Russian emigre pioneer of American radio and head of RCA. What was brought together by this business arrangement was experience in radio manufacture, finance for large-scale investiment and development such as Baird could not match, and advanced research in electronics. EMI had already in 1932 demonstrated its high definition television system which used not a mechanical method but an electronic scanning device. It had been able to make this development by drawing on research which went back to pre-revolutionary Russia where a group of scientists had worked on the development of the cathode ray tube. One of their number, Zworykin, had emigrated to the United States where he joined RCA, while one of his collaborators, Shoenberg, joined the Marconi Company before moving to EMI as head of a team of brilliant researchers. Baird made a desperate attempt to modify his scanning method to meet the challenge of this powerful adversary but it was becoming clear that electronic scanning must prevail. His paranoia had meantime not been helped by the attitude of the BBC which was, as it seemed to Baird, alternately helpful and obstructive. What he was up against was a mixture of scepticism - the chief administrative officer of the BBC thought that the cinema, 'so cheap and so perfect and so universal in its appeal', must triumph over television - and of more justifiable caution on the part of the BBC's engineers who were unimpressed by Baird's wilder claims. On another level, he was confronted by the impenetrable wall which the BBC had become expert in presenting to outsiders. The BBC itself was unwilling to make the final decision between the two systems. A government enquiry was therefore set up to decide the issue. It decided that low definition television, like Baird's, had no real future. This was effectively a death blow to Baird's ambitions, for he was unable to compete in further developments with EMI and its associated interests. When television transmissions began in 1936 both the Baird and the EMI systems were used side by side; but in less than a year it was decided that the EMI system should be adopted. Baird lost out because he did not have the financial resources to switch his research, to acquire patents or to invest the kind of money EMI had at its disposal for research - £180,000 a year in the mid-thirties, which would be the equivalent today to something like £3 million.

As for the control of television, the committee was certain that it should not come under a separate organisation or under any of the firms which had applied for television licences for experimental transmissions. 'The view,' it reported, 'has been held that when television has reached such a stage of development that it would be suitable for a public service, it would probably be found preferable that such a service would be undertaken by the BBC as an adjunct to their broadcasting service.' This view was contested by the General Electric Company, which argued that there should be 'responsible and substantial companies' operating 'on certain wavelengths in certain areas'. This, as we shall see, was a forecast of the pattern of commercial television when it was introduced in 1955. The Newspaper Proprietors' Association was firmly in favour of the BBC on grounds of self-interest, provided that there were 'no forms of advertising by means of what are known as sponsored programmes', which might attract advertising revenue away from the press. Once again, for solid reasons, business interests favoured the concept of public service.

When it did start in 1936, as the first regular public service in the world, BBC television found itself operating under the ethos established by Reith and as 'an adjunct' to BBC radio, with which it shared a clearly formulated social mission. This was, in general, to uplift the British nation whether it was in terms of how people spoke their native tongue - the model, BBC English, was a particular version of educated South-East English - or of what they should find interesting or improving. The real contribution of the BBC to writing, in the shape of radio plays commissioned, or to music by its patronage of composers and performers, is indisputable; but the prevailing tone of its broadcasts was determinedly middle-class. It was an organisation which resisted the introduction of trade unions and which was staffed in large part by men and women who felt the idea of trade unionism distasteful. Pre-war television was aimed at a small and affluent audience in London and the Home Counties, which had not been affected by the depression and mass unemployment. In the South-East prosperity based on the boom in building and light industry and in consumer goods like refrigerators and radios and the car industry financed the purchase of sets. The programmes the viewers watched were dominated by the concept of the West End show, of the revue and the kind of entertainment which was the middle-class audience's idea of a night out. Politics, national or international, on the other hand, was not a topic which the BBC expected its audiences for television or radio to take an interest in. Pressures from government, allied to Reith's own caution, ensured that during the period of the rise of fascism in Germany, Italy and Spain, and of Stalinism in the Soviet Union there was no thorough, continuing discussion in the media of the most important political themes of the day. Nor did the programmes which were transmitted necessarily meet the needs of the audience. Many were turned away by middle-class accents, middle-class interests and middle-class taste and standards. In the pre-war period, 66 per cent of the radio audience tuned in at weekends to foreign commercial stations broadcasting from Luxembourg, Paris and Normandy, which provided a less austere diet than Reith's Sabbatarian programmes - entertainment on Sunday, jazz and information about the pools. (It took the Second World War to persuade the BBC that, in the interest of the morale of the troops, the taboo on Sunday entertainment should be broken.) It was this truant section of the audience which in 1955 was to welcome on commercial television entertainment programmes and personalities with whom it had long been familiar on commercial radio from abroad.

When the television service was re-activated in 1946, having been closed down during the war because it was feared that its transmitters might act as direction-finders for enemy aircraft, it found BBC radio suspicious of its rival medium. There was still a large radio audience for programmes like Tommy Handley's *ITMA* or the *Goon Show*, but fear of losing this audience grew among radio producers as, in the fifties, television licences began to increase by a million a year and radio licences to decrease by the same number. Television was benefiting from the post-war boom, presided over by successive Tory governments, in a Britain saved (they hoped) from socialism and bound for an era of unlimited prosperity. But although television was rising into ascendancy as the most important of the mass media, BBC television was going through a difficult phase within the institution. Control of policy and finance was firmly in the hands of BBC executives in Broadcasting House although television production and transmissions went on at Alexandra Palace some miles away in North London. Physical distance was less important, however, than the fact that management at Broadcasting House was unsympathetic towards television and went to extraordinary lengths to hamper its development. Artists were actively discouraged from appearing on television. Television producers were warned that they must be even more careful than radio producers lest they affront the family audience; thus in 1949 the head of television wardrobes was warned by memo against the dangers of over-exposure of the human body. But most damaging of all was the tight control exercised by radio news over television newscasts; here the dead hand of Broadcasting House was felt at its heaviest. Attempts to provide film coverage of news, to advance television journalism and mount current affairs programmes were systematically blocked. What motivated BBC management in their obstructive tactics was their knowledge that something must be done to bring radio up-to-date; their inability to see how this might be done; and their fear of competition from television, a mass medium which apparently had a peculiar power over its audiences.

It was a period when the BBC was suffering a reaction from the immense prestige it had acquired as the 'voice of the nation' during the Second World War, when its importance as a source of information and as an instrument of social cohesion had been immense. Now in the post-war era it was showing signs of complacency. High principles had degenerated into stuffiness. There were too many executives who still lived in the aura of wartime and pre-war broadcasting. Even the new and growing medium of television was in the post-war period by no means a startling innovator. The BBC's love of animals, of zoos, of children's programmes and of brains trusts, was strongly represented in the programme schedules alongside good drama and the first attempts at television documentaries. A beginning had been made with current affairs programmes such as *Panorama*, but it was not until commercial television began in 1955 that *Panorama* became a weekly programme. What was happening, in fact, was that the consensus which had approved the establishment of the Corporation was crumbling under attack from a number of quarters. The attack was lead by financial and commercial interests.

One important difference from 1926 was that whereas then business interests had been unwilling to invest in what was an entertainments industry - cinema attendances had slumped that year - and were perfectly happy for the British Broadcasting Corporation to provide programmes while they sold the receivers, in the early 1950s they scented the beginning of the consumer society and guessed the profits to be made from television advertising. Between 1951 and 1955 the number of private cars rose from two and a quarter million to three and a quarter million; the number of television sets from one million to five million and the number of telephones from five million to six million. The 1950s saw the launching of new brands of detergents with the aid of massive advertising campaigns; advertising expenditure as a whole was to rise steadily in the first years of the decade. Although many of those who came forward as the protagonists of commercial television denied any direct involvement in the advertising business and claimed to be fighting only in the name of 'freedom', the strong support given to their campaign by prominent Tory MPs was natural and inevitable. There was the possibility of economic advantage from the introduction of television based on something like the American model, which had always been commercial; the Tory party logically supported such economic motives.

One of the first formal gestures towards the breaking of the BBC's monopoly and its replacement by commercial television came from the Tory politician, Selwyn Lloyd, later to be Foreign Minister at the time of the Suez invasion, who in 1951 put the case for commercialisation in a dissenting paper which he attached to the report of the Beveridge Committee, of which he had been a member and which the government had set up to consider the future of broadcasting. The majority of the committee wished to maintain the BBC's monopoly but recognised that it was under attack on a number of grounds. One body of right-wing critics saw a danger in 'excessive power over men's thoughts concentrated in a single organisation'; a Liberal group saw a danger in the excessive size of the Corporation and its unwieldiness; yet another group of critics represented regional cultural minorities which resented central control from London. Another group which objected to the monopoly with more cause than most were those broadcasting professionals who 'whether as employees or independent performers and writers ... fear the power of a monopoly over their own lives'. If a writer, actor or performer, producer or director fell foul of the BBC, they pointed out, they had no alternative employer; this led to self-censorship and undue caution in performance and programme-making. Then there were those who, like Churchill harboured the mad suspicion that the BBC was run by a red conspiracy. While the grounds for the campaign were the straightforward Tory ones of fostering 'individual enterprise' and 'individual freedom', some of the animus which found expression in it must be put down to the fact that the BBC had, as an institution, developed a mandarin aloofness and apparent unwillingness to admit any shortcomings. It was a protective tactic which gave rise to the nickname of Auntie BBC. The campaign for real financial and commercial interests was fed by resentments of the BBC's haughty behaviour and imperviousness to criticism. However, in spite of the hostile views expressed to it, the majority of the Beveridge Committee came to the conclusion that broadcasting should remain the prerogative of a single corporation: the BBC. On the question of advertising the committee found, again by a majority, that 'there are ample means of advertising goods otherwise than on the ether' (a curiously old-fashioned and unscientific expression) and that 'to admit advertisements there would sooner or later endanger the traditions of public service, high standards and impartiality which have been built up over 25 years'. These views were naturally accepted by the Labour government of the day; but, when a few months later in 1951, a Conservative government came to power under Churchill, it speedily announced that it had 'come to the conclusion that in the expanding field of television provision should be made to permit some element of competition'. It would be necessary, however, the government statement went on, to introduce safeguards against possible abuses; a controlling body would be required for this purpose and for exercising 'a general insight over programmes'. Curiously enough the new commercial service was not at this planning stage considered to be fitted to broadcast political or religious programmes, which are expressly denied to it.

The government statement was the signal for the opening of an extraordinary campaign by the commercial and political interests involved - one which was described by the liberal newspaper, *The News Chronicle*, as 'perhaps the most remarkable exhibition of political lobbying this country has ever seen - for there has been no disguise of the commercial interests involved'. As a historian of the campaign has ironically remarked 'the pioneers (of commercial television) and their collaborators were fortunate that their political principles coincided with their career and financial interests'. The supporters of commercial television set up a Popular Television Association whose aim was to demonstrate that the people of Britain were deeply committed to the concept. Its members included, as president, the Earl of Derby, landowner and ex-coal owner, Somerset Maugham, the writer, Alec Bedser, the cricketer, A.J.P. Taylor, the maverick historian and Canon Collins, soon to be prominent in CND. One of the services the Association offered was this: that 'if any members would like draft letters to send to their local papers, we will gladly supply them'. The identical letter, expressing the people's will to have commercial television, appeared in 22 newspapers, with a variety of signatures but always the same address. The extreme right-wing Society for Individual Freedom was enlisted in the cause of liberty for big business, as was Aims of Industry, which today issues monitoring reports on television output on both channels and draws its subscriber's attention to marxist and other dangerous tendencies in programmes. On the side of the BBC was the National Television Society, launched by a letter to *The Times*, whose members included Lord Halifax, Foreign Secretary in the Chamberlain government at the time of Munich, the Liberal peeress, Lady Violet Bonham-Carter, and Tom O'Brien, the right-wing Chairman of the TUC and General Secretary of NATKE. The press, mindful of its own advertising revenue, was in general opposed to commercialisation of the medium. The establishment, as is apparent from the names attached to the rival organisations mentioned above, was deeply split. The public debate in the press and the debates in both Houses of Parliament produced a number of astonishing arguments from the objection of a Conservative peer that commercial advertising would allow the Communist Party to buy time on the air to the argument advanced by Profumo, who was a leading figure in pushing for commercial television, that 'programmes will not be in the hands of the advertisers but will be in the hands of the people'. The Labour Party almost unanimously supported the BBC but waged its campaign not in the form of an attack on the business interests, which hoped to do extremely well out of commercial television and its exploitation of consumers, but on the grounds that in the place of the BBC's Children's Hour - 'properly presented and planned in the interests of children and *of no one else*' - what would be screened was 'the "sensational" and "stunt" type of programme'. Herbert Morrison, the former leader of the LCC and Labour front-bencher threatened that if commercial television were introduced Labour would abolish on its return to power. But when asked their opinion by the Gallup opinion poll a majority of Labour voters expressed themselves in favour of two channels - one BBC and one commercial. The identification of the BBC with the establishment in the minds of many of the licence-holders was probably an important element in influencing their opinions. Conservative and Liberal voters were less enthusiastic.

The outcome of the parliamentary debate was not in any real doubt. Reith in the House of Lords delivered himself of what was counter-productive and empty rhetoric: 'Somebody introduced dog-racing into England; we know who for he is proud of it and proclaims it in the columns of *Who's Who*' - some fellow peer no doubt ·cringed - 'And somebody introduced Christianity and printing and the uses of electricity. And somebody introduced smallpox, bubonic plague and the Black Death into this country. Someone is minded now to introduce sponsored broadcasting into this country'. This was moral indignation divorced from concrete analysis of the effects of introducing a system which must maximise audiences for advertisers, degenerated into farce. Hailsham argued passionately and legalistically that the BBC could not be attacked as being monopolistic for it 'was not a monopoly in the accepted sense of the word since it sold nothing'. The Lord Chancellor produced a line of Tory populism asking: 'Must we not give the people what they want because they might want something that is not good for them?'

The legislation duly passed through parliament. In 1954 the Television Act became law and set up an authority to provide 'television broadcasting services additional to those of the BBC and of high quality'.

6 Commercial Television

The organisation created to provide these programmes was the Independent Television Authority; the network it controlled came to be called Independent Television (ITV). The adjective 'independent' was deeply resented by the BBC, whose executives maintained that the Corporation was the only truly 'independent' body because it did not depend on commercial interests for its revenue. For a considerable time, therefore, it was a BBC house rule that the competing network was to be described, when it had to be mentioned at all, as 'commercial television'. The fact of the matter is that in political terms the ITA was just as independent or as dependent as the BBC, for the minister to whom the Authority was responsible - the Postmaster General - might, as in the case of the BBC, give notice in writing for the Authority to 'refrain from broadcasting any matter or classes of matter' specified by him. He could further lay down the hours of broadcasting. He also had powers to sack any members of the Authority. What was lacking, in the case of the ITA, was that power of indirect control through the regulation of the licence fee which we have seen obtains where the BBC is concerned. One fundamental and striking difference between the BBC and the ITA lay in another direction; it was that, although the Authority was to broadcast programmes - and was therefore responsible for ensuring that a reasonable signal was available to viewers - it did not itself have the responsibility for originating them. As far as coverage of the country was concerned, there was a further difference between the two broadcasting organisations: the BBC's aim has always been, whether in radio or television, to give national coverage even of remote and thinly populated areas of the country; the ITA from the beginning concentrated on highly populated areas from which correspondingly high advertising revenues could be extracted. Parts of Scotland, for example, are to this day not covered by an ITV signal.

One of the principal duties laid upon the Authority was to satisfy themselves 'so far as possible' that the programmes they broadcast included 'nothing ... which offends against good taste or decency or is likely to encourage or incite to crime or to lead to disorder or to be offensive to public feeling'. There was no corresponding injunction in either the BBC's Charter or in the Licence granted to it by the Postmaster General - nor is there today; what does exist is a letter from the Chairman of the BBC, written in 1964 (which as we shall see was an important date for British television) undertaking to ensure that 'so far as possible' BBC programmes would contain 'nothing ... which offends against good taste, decency etc'. In the same letter an undertaking was given that the BBC would treat controversial subjects 'with due impartiality', a duty laid upon the ITA by the Television Act 1954 which obliges the Authority 'to ensure that the programmes maintain a proper balance in their subject-matter and a high general standard of quality; that any news given ... is presented with due accuracy and impartiality', 'that due impartiality is preserved ... as respects matters of political or industrial controversy or in relation to current public policy' (the concept of 'impartiality' is by no means as unproblematic as the Act suggests); and that 'no matter designed to serve the interests of any political party is included in the programmes'. There is an interesting nuance in the difference between the obligations laid on the ITA and the self-imposed restraints proposed by the Chairman of the BBC, which reflect that policy of complicity established by Reith at the time of the General Strike. Further duties laid upon the ITA were to ensure that 'proper proportions of the recorded and other matter ... included in the programmes are of British origin and British performance' (a clause aimed - not very successfully - at the wholesale importation of American material).

The programmes were, as we have seen, not to be provided by the Authority - that was an obligation undertaken by contractors who had 'the right and duty' to provide programmes to be broadcast over the Authority's transmitters. For this right the contractors were to pay a rental, thus providing the finance for the Authority to operate its transmitters, pay for its staff and for other running costs. The contractors, for their part, were to be financed and to draw their profits from accepting commercial advertising in programmes. There is in the 1954 Act one long and involved clause which lays down that 'nothing shall be included in any programme broadcast by the Authority ... which states, suggests or implies ... that any part of any programme ... has been supplied or suggested by any advertiser'. What this means is that safeguards were built into the act to prevent anything in the nature of sponsorship, the system on which American television depended. It was a system which politicians on both sides of the House of Commons had seen in action; what they saw of American television had persuaded them that sponsorship was responsible for many of its obvious defects and they were determined that no comparable system should be introduced in Britain.

The drawback of sponsorship lay in the fact that the sponsor, having put up all or part of the money to fund a television series, could exert editorial influence on its content with two aims: one was that nothing should be seen or said on the screen that might conceivably bring the sponsor's product into disrepute; the other, that nothing should be included in the programme that might alienate any of the potential purchasers of the product. The United States is a country of many religious and racial groups and of many strong sectional interests. Nothing might be included in a sponsored programme which might offend any of these groups or sectional interests. (Class interests were, in the view of the sponsors non-existent.) The result was a flow of blandness calculated to upset no one; if social issues were raised in any programme the solution had to be one of reconciliation - a demonstration that although people might have personal problems all was well. One historian of American television quotes the case of *Man Against Crime*, which was being produced by CBS at the very time when the debate over commercial television was beginning in Britain. The series was sponsored by Camel Cigarettes, who issued instructions to the writers employed on the series required them 'not to have the heavy or any disreputable person smoking a cigarette'. They were not to 'associate the smoking of cigarettes with undesirable scenes or situations plot-wise'. Cigarettes were to be puffed gracefully and not dragged on as if to steady nerves. Doctors, who were becoming worried about possible links between smoking and cancer, were to be shown only 'in the most commendable light'. There were other instructions concerned with plots and storylines. 'It has been found', writers were informed, 'that we retain audience interest best when our story is concerned with murder. Therefore, although other crimes may be introduced, somebody must be murdered, preferably early, with the threat of more violence to come.' The hero must be threatened early and often; his love life should 'not stop the forward motion of the picture' but the plot should feature at least one attractive woman. Stories of such pressures from sponsors - pressures which were aimed at a maximisation of audience without regard to the quality of the programmes - were common at the time of the British television debate. Clause 4 (6), quoted above was the result.

There were further controls on advertisements on British television. They had to be 'clearly distinguishable as such and recognisably separate from the rest of the programme' - another attempt to avoid the excesses of some American television advertising in which a newscaster or presenter in a discussion programme would suddenly switch roles to deliver 'a message from our sponsor' exhorting viewers to buy Brand X; they were 'not to be inserted except at the beginning or end of the programme or in natural breaks therein' - a further attempt to avoid an American practice, which was that of interrupting a programme so often as to destroy its continuity. (What was or was not a 'natural break' was to become the subject of some debate.) There was to be agreement between the Authority and the Postmaster General as to the spacing of advertisements and the kind of programmes 'which shall in particular include the broadcast of any religious service' in which advertisements might not be inserted. Over and above such controls on advertising the Authority was granted powers to require the programme contractor to provide in advance scripts and information about the nature of projected programmes. These were, on the face of it, wide-ranging powers - if the Authority chose to exercise them; this they did only half-heartedly.

Although the campaign for commercial television had awakened impassioned support in certain quarters, including the advertising lobby and the set-manufacturers, when the Authority invited offers for the franchises allowing contractors to make programmes, the response was rather poor; only 25 financial groups applied for the 14 franchises into which the Authority had divided the country. It had, explained the Authority, the choice between a 'unitary' system, which would - like the BBC with its strong centralisation and its limited regional devolution of money and resources - have been centred on London, and a 'plural' system, a definition which suggested that there might be a plurality of programme choices. Great play was made by the Authority of the argument that by opting for a 'plural' system they were serving local interests and filling a gap which the BBC had undoubtedly neglected to an astonishing degree. In theory the 'plural' system should have been a federation of equals but it did not take long after ITV started broadcasting in September 1955 for certain of the contractors - called the Big Four - to establish dominating positions in the network. This came about because of their financial power and the richness of their franchises, and because of the amount they had invested in studios and other equipment as well as in staff (often tempted across from the BBC by offers of better wages and salaries than the Corporation believed it could afford). They were Rediffusion Television, the London week-day company; Associated Television (ATV), which provided London's weekend programmes and week-day programmes for the Midlands; ABC Television, the programme contractor for weekends in the North and in the Midlands; and Granada, responsible for weekday programmes in the North. The ten others were regional companies with limited resources and little say in the councils of the network.

One possible reason for the limited competition for the franchises was that not everyone was persuaded that commercial television was financially viable in Britain. The *Daily Telegraph* questioned whether 'advertisers will find this new medium worthwhile and will pay enough to make the hiring companies solvent'. The *Manchester Guardian* (as it then was) doubted whether the advertising revenue would be able to support a competitive system. *The Times* and *The Economist* were both pessimistic. In this pessimism there was naturally a reflection of concern that the new network might affect the advertising revenue of the press; but it was also an echo, in economic terms, of the doubts within the establishment as to the advisability of the whole venture - doubts which reflected not only divergent economic interests but different ideas about how a capitalist society should inform, instruct and entertain itself. To these must be added a certain patrician suspicion of show-business and an element of anti-semitism. For the first two or three years of ITV it seemed as if the pessimists were to be proved correct. Associated Television with the immensely rich London franchise lost nearly £3 million, which so alarmed one of the important shareholders - Associated Newspapers, owners of the *Daily Mail*, the *Sketch* and other publications - that they sold their shares and got out. In the present-day companies it is still possible to hear from executives who were involved at this early stage in their history of cash-flow difficulties - of one company having to beg another for money to pay its staff at the end of the week and of deep fears that the whole project might founder. But by

1958 Associated Newspapers had reason to regret its loss of nerve; in that year Associated Rediffusion made a profit of over £4 million. Its example was followed by ATV, which from 1959 began to make annual profits of £5 million. It has rightly been said by one observer that 'not since the days of the East India Company were fortunes made so easily'. The advertisers and the advertising agencies were willing to pay the rates demanded by the contractors; members of the public, caught in the consumer boom, paid for the profits of the television companies every time they bought a packet of detergent or a tin of convenience food in the local supermarket. Nor was it only the big four who found themselves to be millionaire companies; smaller companies, including Scottish Television, whose franchise covered the thickly populated industrial belt of Central Scotland shared in the bonanza to such an extent that Lord Thomson, Chairman of the company and future owner of *The Times*, in a famous phrase described a commercial television franchise as 'a licence to print money'. The wealth extracted from commercial television did not flow into the pockets of 'the people' whom Profumo had cynically suggested would control commercial television; nor did it go into improving the quality of programmes. British capitalism had found a huge and untapped source of wealth and proceeded to exploit it with almost total disregard for equality of programmes or for the pious terms of the Television Act.

That the profitability of the companies has never been in real doubt is evident from the very large sums which they proceeded to siphon off into other activities. This process of 'diversification' has led the companies to have interests in spheres remote from television, which rapidly became an industry generating cash for investment elsewhere. This, the companies said, was a necessary precaution since the contracts were for only a limited period - ten years in the first instance; steps had therefore to be taken to cover the programme contractors against the possibility of their franchises not being renewed. So Granada became involved in book publishing, bingo halls, motorway services, music publishing, cinemas, property and TV rental; ATV extended into feature films, theatres, cinemas, music publishing, record companies, property. The result was that an extraordinary interlocking network of interests was set up - a subject to which we shall return later. At this point what we should note is that television rapidly became very big business and that the criteria of big business were applied to the production and the marketing of programmes, which were packaged like the products which they helped to advertise and judged primarily by their ability to attract mass audiences. For their part, the men who ran the companies made no attempt to conceal the view that profitability and mass audiences were inseparable.

This avowal they made in evidence presented to the Pilkington Committee, presided over by the paternalistic glass manufacturer, Sir Harry Pilkington, and set up by the Conservative government in 1960 to consider the future of the broadcasting services in the United Kingdom. The membership of the Committee was in no sense radical, although the inclusion on it of Richard Hoggart, whose book, *The Uses of Literacy*, an important early contribution to cultural studies and to the debate concerning working-class culture, was the recognition on someone's part of the relevance of such studies to the mass media of radio and television. The compelling reasons for the setting up of the committee included the fact that the BBC was pressing for permission to start a second television channel and that, above all, in view of the record of ITV it was necessary to review its situation in good time for any changes to be made before the franchises came up for renewal in 1965. The Committee made its report in 1962. On the evidence submitted to it, it stated, there was widespread dissatisfaction with television 'because the range of subjects dealt with was too narrow, because within the range there was not sufficient variety in treatment and because the range represented at peak viewing hours was markedly narrower than the overall range'. Other reasons for disquiet quoted by the Committee included the triviality of television; 'the preoccupation in many programmes with the superficial and the cheaply sensational'; violence and the portrayal 'of low standards and behaviour'. The Committee did not specify which groups or organisations had formulated these complaints. An examination of the list of bodies and persons who submitted evidence to the Committee shows, however, that it included a number of interests and lobbies whose defence of 'traditional values' could easily combine moral disapproval with reactionary political attitudes. What is certain is that the Committee, from its own liberal consensus point of view, found the charges proven against both the BBC and ITV companies - 'the BBC is not blameless' they commented; but their broad conclusion was that the BBC's television service sinned to a lesser degree and was 'a successful realisation of broadcasting as defined in the Charter'. It is notable that there is nowhere in the Report any analysis of the concepts of impartiality, of the concepts underlying the BBC's news value, or of the social and political ideology of the output of either the Corporation or the ITV companies. Indeed the concept of ideology is foreign to the Committee for the simple reason that a committee working within the terms of the dominant ideology of our society would see nothing to challenge in it.

It was for the ITA and the programme contractors that the Committee reserved its strongest condemnations. There was, it stated, a widespread feeling that the Authority was 'not in effective control of commercial television'. The Committee itself rejected the Authority's stated satisfaction with the service provided by ITV. One of the root causes of the shortcomings of the service seemed to the Committee to lie in the fact that 'the two purposes of independent television do not coincide'. It proceeded to explain why. 'Since the commercial product, the saleable product of the contractors is not the programmes but the advertising time, the commercial rewards will derive from making that product as desirable as possible to those who want it, an aim largely incompatible with the purposes of broadcasting' as the Committee saw them. One opinion expressed by the Authority clearly nettled the Committee - the opinion that the commonly held view that television exerted a high degree of influence on society was exaggerated. The Chairman of the Authority, an ex-Foreign Office official, had gone so far as to tell the Committee that society would largely be what it was - with or without television. This was not a view shared by the Committee, which called for a code to be drawn up by the Authority on the representation of violence similar to that which the BBC had itself formulated. It also attacked quizzes in which valuable prizes were offered for little effort and programmes which ridiculed and humiliated ordinary people for the amusement of the television audience. In general the Committee felt that 'the Authority's policies did not sufficiently reckon with the influence of television on values and moral standards generally' and that this was clear from 'many of the independent television's programmes of entertainment'. There was criticism, too, of the amount and timing of serious programmes - too few and too late. It was during discussion of this point that one company after another admitted that their aim was to seek the largest audience. Lord Thomson had said, with his usual frankness: 'Because the advertisers pay for viewers it is inevitable that it (commercial television) serve the majority.'

The Report of the Committee was widely believed to have

been largely framed by Hoggart. It was highly critical of television within the framework of consensus morality and consensus ideology. Thus the Committee was at some pains to explain that, when putting forward its recommendations for the reform of commercial television, it was not attempting to 'nationalise it'. Yet they were forced to come back to the fact that the main discipline the contractors recognised was 'the discipline of the profit and loss account'; from this it followed that their natural inclination was to pursue as their main purpose the sale of advertising time - a private objective which did not 'coincide with the primary and essential public objective, the best possible service of broadcasting.' The companies' large profits 'derive from the use of a facility which is part of the public, and not the private domain'; this was unsatisfactory, because it meant that these profits derived from the grant on the public behalf of a highly-privileged concession. The use of broadcasting time was the use of a national asset. It therefore proposed that the Authority should plan the programming for ITV; should receive all the advertising revenue; that the programme companies should produce and sell to the Authority programmes to fill the schedule. None of these recommendations was acted on by the Conservative government.

As for the BBC, the Committee recommended that it should remain 'the main instrument of broadcasting in the United Kingdom'; it should also be allowed to start a second television channel. The approval of the BBC's actions, policies and programmes was general. The Committee praised the professionalism which they found there, by which they meant 'not so much a competence, a mastery of techniques' as at executive levels, 'where both principles and the public interest are interpreted and re-interpreted, a recognition of what - in terms of programme planning and performance - is needed to give substance to these principles'. In other words, the BBC understood its social duty and was able to plan its service in that light. The Pilkington Report was received inside the BBC, on the one hand, with a certain smug satisfaction and, on the other, with a niggling feeling that the Report had erred on the side of gilding the lily.

In 1964 the Conservative government passed a new Television Act which increased the powers and duties of the Authority, specifying that the programme contractors must draw up a programme schedule in consultation with the Authority and that the

Authority could give instructions as to the inclusion or exclusion of any item in it. The Authority would give final approval to the schedule. It was also required to draw up a code governing the showing of violence, particularly when large numbers of young people might be watching, and in general to impose requirements as to standards and practice in programme-making. It was also given the express power to impose 'inhibitions and restrictions' on the programme contractors. Although these provisions were widely welcomed at the time and although they did put an end to some of the worst and most cynically exploitative programmes, they were in due course - over the question of Ireland and the role of British imperialism there as well as over other topics which were thought might be 'offensive' (to whom? why?) - to form the basis of the censorship exercised by the Authority. For in the sixties, political censorship in the commercial companies became stricter. Some companies employed their own internal censors, who were not programme-makers or programme executives but invigilators who watched film in the viewing theatre or the editing room and offered their view that 'the Authority will not like that' or 'that should come out'. This was the period when the Authority effectively stopped an episode in a drama series which showed a Conservative MP - a fictional character - in a situation involving young girls and a swimming pool. The echoes of the Profumo scandal were too close to allow that to pass during the run-up to a general election. Another drama programme on a military prison was kept off the air because it might offend the military; the prison was named in the title as 'the Glasshouse' - the army slang for the British military detention centre. A remake, placing the action in a Ruritanian country, was still felt to be too dangerous by the Authority. The programme never went out. What had begun as a measure against exploitative programmes becames a social and political weapon.

One remarkable innovation followed from the Television Act 1964. It was the direct tax on the programme contractors which came to be known as 'the Levy'. This was an additional payment over and above the rentals which the companies already paid to the Authority; the proceeds from the Levy the Authority was required by the Act to pay into the Exchequer. The rates laid down in the Act were that the first £1.5 million of the advertising receipts would not be subject to this new tax - which was, of course, a payment over and above normal income tax; that the rate for the next £6 million would be 25 per cent; and for anything over that figure 45 per cent. The fact that a Conservative government proposed and supported this provision in the Act is an indication of the dimensions of the scandal which the profits - personal and corporate - amassed by commercial television during its first few years in existence represented. This was 'the unacceptable face of capitalism'. The programme contractors had made the mistake - not of making very large profits - but of making them through the use of what was regarded as a public medium and of boasting about them. The profits made from speculation in the City by trading on 'futures' in foodstuffs - speculating that is to say on the prices of crops not yet gathered and on the essentials of life - are tolerated because the mechanisms and operations involved in such transactions are normally concealed from public view. Television was not sheltered in this way. Therefore the contractors had to be penalised; 'the discipline of the profit and loss account' was used against them by politicians whose aim was to preserve the profits system. It took a Labour government to feel pity for the contractors. Return on capital in 1968-69 was around 40 per cent; in 1969-70 it fell to a mere 25 per cent and then, in the following year to 10 per cent. This temporary fall in profitablity led to cries of hardship from the companies and induced the Labour Postmaster General to reduce the size of the Levy - a step which may be explained in part by the fact that Labour voters watch ITV and in part by the close links between the Wilson circle and show business interests. Since then another Labour government has again tempered the edge of the Levy by calculating it not on the companies' advertising revenue but on their profits. As the IBA Handbook puts it: 'A profits-based Levy is more acceptable than the previous one on spending income because it allows the system to adjust more easily to fluctuations without having as severe an effect on the quality of the service as the previous arrangement.' The 'effect on the quality of the service' is a muted reference to the fact that when profits began to fall the first item in the companies' budgets to be cut was programme cost. Today the companies are still immensely profitable.

One important effect of the act was to compel the Authority to take a greater part in the control of programme scheduling. This is now achieved through a series of committees. The IBA's views on policy are passed on to the companies by the Programme Policy Committee, which is presided over by the Chairman of the Authority. It is attended by the company heads and programme controllers and by senior Authority staff. Co-operation on programming between the companies is worked out by the Network Programme Committee on which there are two representatives of the Authority as well as programme chiefs from the companies. The detailed working out of the network schedules, which is dominated by the large companies, is decided by the Programme Controllers' Group, which meets every week. They put together a basic schedule which is offered to each of the programme companies as a basic framework on which they can build their own schedules. This, in the case of the smaller regional companies, means generally the inclusion of some local magazine programmes or local documentary, since they have neither the money nor the resources to embark on large-scale productions. Under this system, and mindful of the criticisms levelled at it in the Pilkington Report which had stated roundly that 'it had misconceived its relationship with the programme contractors; that it saw itself as an advocate of them; that it excused and defended rather than controlled them', the Authority has used its powers to 'mandate' certain programme such as *World in Action*, *TV Eye* and documentary programmes. Mandated programmes must be included in the schedules at specified times and cannot be put out at times when there will be very small audiences.

The Authority's powers were demonstrated in a different way when the franchises were re-allocated in 1968. This time there was no lack of applicants for what was rightly seen as the opportunity to participate in a thriving industry. The Authority used the occasion to re-arrange the areas covered by the franchise. Thus it split 'Granadaland' into two, giving the eastern half of the area to Yorkshire Television and allowing new business interests to have their share of the profits. In London it refused to renew the franchise of Rediffusion Television, which was dominated by business people who had allowed their view that television was concerned with the manufacture of products and that the only criterion of success was the ratings to be pushed too far for the Authority to be able to overlook the appallingly low level of the programmes. The company with the Welsh franchise, which had obstinately refused to transfer its operation from London to Cardiff also lost its franchise to a new company, Harlech Television (HTV). ABC merged with some of the financial interests represented by the defunct Rediffusion to form Thames Television, serving the London area from Monday to Friday afternoon; London Weekend Television was given the remainder of the week. It would not be apparent to a viewer today that LWT made its bid for the franchise on the basis of a document which stated that the applicants were 'convinced that there are new ways of attracting a mass audience that are not being explored and that this is particularly true of weekend programming'; that they believed that no audience is 'exclusively mass or minority'; and proposed that the weekend would see plays from living writers, science programmes and news in depth. The company began operations with a talented group of programme-makers, many recruited from the BBC; most of them, including the Controller of Programmes, had disappeared within a year. The policy of the company was then re-phrased in the following terms by the news programme head: 'The first duty of a commercial station is to survive.' Although the programme policy pursued by the company from that date on bore very little relationship to the promises made to the Authority, that body did not see fit to intervene. It was at this time that the Chairman of the Authority, a former Labour Chief Whip, stated the old philosophy of commercial television afresh: 'I find it a little difficult to understand criticism of programme content when currently we are getting seventeen programmes out of the Top Twenty almost every week.'

7 The Fourth Channel

From 1955 until 1980 the pattern of British television has remained essentially the same. It can be summarised as follows. On the one hand there is the BBC, a London dominated institution, funded by licence revenue and specifically instructed by its Charter that money derived from any source - profits from the sale of *Radio Times*, sale of programmes abroad, or merchandising (recordings of signature tunes, T-shirts, toys associated with programmes) - must be ploughed back into broadcasting. It considers itself to be 'the national instrument of broadcasting' and has been referred to by the Home Secretary in the Thatcher government, who is the minister responsible for broadcasting, as 'arguably the single most important cultural organisation in the nation'. On the other hand, there is the Independent Broadcasting Authority, which controls a federal system of programme contractors who, in return for the payment of a rental to the Authority, have the duty to provide programmes for the Authority to broadcast and the right to collect advertising in their franchise areas. The Authority exacts from the contractors what are described in the Television Act as 'additional payments' deducted from the advertising receipts of the programme contractors and paid into the Treasury; these 'additional payments' are the Levy. In 1980 the Thatcher government introduced into parliament legislation to enable the Authority to provide what was described in the Bill as a 'Second Television Service'. That there was room in the broadcasting spectrum for such a service had been known for many years. The BBC occupies two channels in the spectrum and the ITV companies another one; during the discussions which led up to the introduction of the legislation, the remaining unoccupied channel was commonly referred to as the Fourth Channel. It was noticeable that although a government decision to go ahead with the new service was long delayed, the set manufacturers had pre-empted matters by labelling the appropriate button on their sets 'ITV2'.

The debate over the precise nature of the service to be provided on the Fourth Channel and who should make the programmes for the service raised all the main issues in broadcasting policy - the question of editorial control, of finance and of organisational structures; the crucial one concerned with the relationship of broadcasting to the state was not among them. That issue was eventually raised by the Home Secretary. As minister responsible for broadcasting he was very clear on the subject, stating that 'the relationship between the government and the broadcasting authorities ... is what television in a free society is all about'.

On the organisational side the debate, which spread over almost a decade, produced a wide range of models, many of which aimed at providing a wider choice for viewers and at the encouragement of experimental and innovatory programme-making. Statements were made stressing the importance of providing access to the medium by groups or individuals outside the established broadcasting institutions; questions were posed about the editorial control of output; proposals emerged ranging from a channel providing access to minority groups to a regional service providing community television, from a new publicly financed service to compete with the BBC to a second commercial channel run by a new set of programme contractors. The bodies and interests involved in the debate were numerous but certain of them clearly had the advantage of established positions within broadcasting: these were the BBC, the IBA and the programme contractors. Of these the BBC was a marginal force because during the period of the debate it was in considerable financial difficulties and had little room for manoeuvre. It might have been expected that the important business interests represented by the advertising industry would have played an important part in the debate. Their part turned out to be a minor one, however. Their main aim was to break the ITV programme contractors' monopoly of the market for television advertising. What they hoped for, therefore, was a system which would introduce an element of competition leading to lower advertising rates. So they advocated competition between two 'general interest' channels - BBC1 and ITV1, both financed by commercial advertising - and the reduction of BBC2 and the Fourth Channel to cultural ghettoes for 'special interests' and 'social and educational programmes'. Their model was never seriously considered and it is difficult to understand why they ever thought it could be realised. The inability of the advertising lobby to influence the course of the debate in any serious way can perhaps be attributed to the immense power and influence of the programme contractors, who were determined to defend their monopoly, but another crucial factor appears to have been that strain of puritanism within the Tory Party which manifested itself in the 1954 debates over the introduction of commercial television. Thus the Tory Home Secretary, in the speech from which we have quoted above, declared that 'competitive advertising on the two channels would inevitably result in a move towards single-minded concentration on maximising the audience with adverse consequences for both of the commercial companies and before long for the BBC as well'. He then added in a frank account of how the profit motive works that this was 'not a criticism of the television companies'. He did not believe that 'they could prevent it if they tried and remain viable'.

The main lobby outside the broadcasting institutions - apart from the advertisers - was made up of 'independent producers', a large numbers of whom came together in the Channel Four Group. The title 'independent' was an ambiguous one. The question was independent of what and of whom? Some of these 'independents' were frustrated entrepreneurs who had found it difficult to sell their programmes and programme ideas to the existing institutions and saw in the Fourth Channel an outlet for their energies and a market for their productions. Like the advertisers they were anxious to break the resistance of a monopolistic situation - a buyer's market in which both BBC and ITV drove hard bargains. These entrepreneurs made uneasy partners for another group of film-makers and television people who were opposed on principle to the commercial exploitation of the new channel seeing in it an opportunity to put on the air programmes which challenged the aesthetic and ideological assumptions of main-stream television. Their attitudes range from radical-liberal to radical-left. What they shared was the optimistic belief that it is possible to work as radicals within the institutions of bourgeois democracy and within the television organisations in particular. They also shared a common underestimation of the strength of the power structures in our society and of the constraints that were bound to be placed on television in an era of political and economic crisis. There were also, overlapping with the radical independents, women's pressure groups who wished the Fourth Channel to be used to improve their sex's opportunities in television, to provide training schemes for women, to put out programmes which would portray women in a wider range of roles than has traditionally been the case and to ensure that regular opportunities were given 'to explore the way women seen themselves and the spectrum of their social and cultural values'. What they had in mind, among other things, were regular programmes for women which transcended the traditional Women's Hour model.

There were also a few - a very few - voices which forcefully maintained that a new television channel was unnecessary; that, given willingness on the part of the BBC and the ITV companies, there was ample air-time to mount innovatory programmes; that in terms of social priorities a fourth television channel came very far down the list; and that experience in other countries showed that more television did not necessarily mean better television.

One proposal which was certainly in itself innovatory was for a National Television Foundation which would broaden output by allowing anyone to bring a project to it - even if it were 'only an idea, a grievance, a cause'; the Foundation would provide the human and material resources to realise the programme. Finance would come from a variety of sources: from a fixed annual levy on advertising; from payments from education authorities; from sponsored programmes. The Foundation would operate under a Charter and through a board of governors chosen partly by government and partly by other institutions, including the trade unions in the broadcasting industry. What was important about the proposal was the idea of an organisation which would - as it were - act as a publisher and, like any other publisher, would not accept responsibility for everything said by its authors (or programme-makers) but would, again like any publisher, be subject to the laws of the land on such matters as libel or contempt of court. This was a model without parallel anywhere in the world and in many ways a very desirable one; the doubts felt by many people who were in principle in favour of it were based on the difficulty of persuading any government to relax its controlling powers over broadcasting. The chances of the basic concept of the Foundation being accepted seemed to increase when the Annan Committee, set up by the Labour government to examine the future of broadcasting, made a firm proposal in its report (published in 1977) that 'an Open Broadcasting Authority be established to take responsibility for the services of the fourth television channel' and to encourage productions which 'say something new in new ways'. These would include educational programmes, programmes made by individual companies (including the ITV contractors) and by independent producers. Finance would come from a number of sources including block advertising - that is to say, periods of up to a half-hour at a fixed spot in the schedules in which commercials are concentrated, this being a common practice on German and Italian television - from sponsored programmes and from educational grants. The mention of sponsored programmes by the Annan Committee and by those who proposed the Foundation was a break with a long tradition in British broadcasting which forbade sponsorship. That it was even considered was an indication of the real financial difficulties facing any non-commercial broadcasting organisation on the one hand and of the increasing tendency on the part of very large firms to carry out prestige advertising by sponsoring cultural events like operas on the other hand. What was even more controversial, in terms of the traditional ground rules of British broadcasting, was the Committee's suggestion that the Open Broadcasting Authority set up to supervise the Fourth Channel would not be required 'to schedule a balanced evening's viewing'. That this did not mean complete publishing freedom was clear, however, from two riders: one of these said that the OBA would have to maintain a balance over a period of time (which no true publisher would feel required to do); the other indicated that if balance were not maintained the Authority would be penalised. This was spelt out clearly: 'If the Authority acquired the reputation of consistently permitting programmes to appear which favoured one particular political interpretation of life, still more if it permitted its service to be taken over by political extremists, it would soon lose its remit from parliament.'

The Labour Party indicated its assent to the terms of the Annan Report but was too concerned with the approaching general election of 1979 to give it any parliamentary attention. Television and broadcasting in general do not interest politicians and they tend to be extremely ignorant about the problems of the media. There was however, urgent need for a decision because the ITV contracts were due for renewal by 1982; the IBA needed to know how to frame the public advertisements inviting tenders for the contracts. So the Tories had to decide on the future of television; it was obvious that the concept of an Open Broadcasting Authority would not appeal to them. In fact the Home Secretary somewhat slightingly dismissed the Annan Report as 'extremely valuable ... and written with wit, charm and style of a high order', and proceeded to disregard its major recommendations. It took the Home Office a considerable time to draft legislation. Meanwhile the IBA, clearly on the basis of close consultations with the government, felt able to make confident statements about how matters were to be arranged. Thus the Director General of the IBA declared that the new channel would encourage innovation, would provide complementary programming to that offered by ITV1 (which implied that the channel would be controlled by the Authority) and that programmes would be provided by 'the unsatisfied talents' in the fifteen ITV companies as well as by independent producers and educational establishments. By this time some of the main contractors such as ATV, Thames Television and Yorkshire Television had set up 'independent' companies to produce film and television programmes; 'independent' producers did not, therefore, necessarily mean the Fourth Channel radicals. As far as the size of audience was concerned the IBA declared that it would be 'perfectly satisfactory' if ITV1 continued to be watched by between 40 and 45 per cent of the viewing public with between 15 and 20 per cent tuning in to the Fourth Channel. (This could naturally only be achieved by detaching part of the audience from BBC TV.) More importantly there was to be no all-out competition between the two commercial channels and no break in the TV companies' monopoly over the selling of advertising time on the air.

What was still obscure was how the new channel was to be financed, a point which clearly presented a problem to the Home Office and possibly to the Tory cabinet. The Annan Report had advocated that the Open Broadcasting Authority should to some extent be financed from government sources. This the Home Secretary turned down as a solution on the grounds that it would be 'potentially dangerous' to create a body dependent to some degree on government finance. What the government favoured was spot advertising - perhaps supplemented by sponsorship and block advertising. But it was made clear that the budget for the fourth channel would not necessarily be dependent on the revenue earned from the commercials it carried. Where then was the extra money to fund it to come from? One obvious source was the advertising revenue of the ITV programme companies; but that would mean a cut in the Levy, those 'extra payments' which the companies pay to the Treasury through the IBA. A cut in receipts to the Treasury, which was put at about £70 million, was not likely to be popular with a government which was slashing expenditure with monetarist zeal. The question was cleared up by the IBA which took the remarkable step of announcing its proposals for 'the new television service to start in the autumn of 1982' - remarkable because there was still no legislation defining the organisation or indeed guaranteeing the existence of the new channel. The money was to be raised, said the Authority, from the ITV programme contractors as a Fourth Channel subscription; the contribution paid by the individual companies were to be computed on the same basis as their IBA rentals. It would amount to something in the order of £60 to £80 million. But the new channel was not to be 'a permanent pensioner of ITV'; in due course it would add between a quarter and a fifth to the total advertising revenue earned by the programme contractors. As for how that revenue was to be collected, the arrangement foreseen was that the ITV contractors would sell airtime on the new channel in their own franchise areas.

As far as the organisation of the channel was concerned the Authority proposed a variant on the pattern of ITV1 with the traditional control mechanisms intact. There was to be no question of greater editorial autonomy for the new service. The

Fourth Channel would be run by a company which would commission and acquire programmes, plan the schedule, appoint and employ staff and operate within the budgets fixed by the Authority. The company would not make programmes itself but acquire them wherever it saw fit. The service it provided would be complementary to ITV1 but it should not be denied the opportunity to draw large audiences. What this means was spelt out in terms in programme 'mix'. The Authority saw the 'mix' on ITV1 continuing as at present while the Fourth Channel merely reversed that 'mix'. What this means is that ITV1 and the Fourth Channel will be planned so that viewers will have little incentive to switch to either BBC channel.

Although the IBA and the programme contractors of ITV had seen things go as they wished and planned, as the country's economic situation started to deteriorate they began to look forward to the new service on the Fourth Channel with some trepidation. The IBA had warned that there was a prospect of 'a cyclical decline in television advertising revenue' from its 1978 peak of £410 million. It followed that expectations that funds would from the start be 'freely and uncritically available' were unlikely to be fulfilled; but this should not, the Authority commented, be a deterrent to the production of good programmes. The programme contractors, for their part, issued warnings about the state of the industry and suggested that a fall in advertising revenue might make it necessary to adjust the scale and nature of the second service; it might be wise, they said, not to stick too firmly to a starting date in 1982. It is a well known tactic of the programme contractors to plead poverty in public from time to time; such protestations are not to be taken too seriously. But the people who have grown rich on the great television bonanza for quarter of a century could see the economic crisis deepening and were perhaps legitimately, wondering whether the boom could continue indefinitely. The BBC had little comment to make on the proposed pattern for the new service. What was clear, however, was the danger that the BBC, as an under-financed organisation unable to pay technicians and other employees the rates which the unions have won from the ITV companies, would be marginalised, in other words, that it would become a diminished institution which in its weakness can be expected to behave in an increasingly deferential way to government. The Home Secretary's reference to its cultural status was small comfort, particularly when in the same breath the minister proposed a new method of agreeing on the BBC's financial requirements. The Home Office, it was announced, was to introduce a new system whereby it would reach an understanding with the BBC about 'the level of expenditure ... likely to be acceptable for each year in a four year planning period'. This appeared to mean that the BBC would submit forecasts of expenditure to a government department for approval so that the Home Secretary could 'satisfy himself, parliament and the licence holders ... about the level of financial provision made for BBC broadcasting'. This was, on the face of it, a serious step towards closer government control.

What the new system for ITV2/Channel 4 achieves is to confirm the programme contractors of ITV as the most important and powerful group in the British television industry. Their financial power had been demonstrated in the summer of 1979 when they stood out for eleven weeks, during which the test card was the only signal transmitted, against the demands of the film and television union, ACTT, for a larger share of the profits of commercial television - profits created by the work of its members. In the end the companies agreed to a compromise which granted the union the bulk of its demands; but in the meantime they were able to live on their reserves whereas the advertising agencies, which provide the commercials from which the programme contractors draw their revenues, were in dire straits. One source of the companies' strength was the extent to which they had diversified - had invested profit in businesses outside the television industry. This step is usually justified on the grounds that it is merely good business sense or, alternatively, that since there is no absolute guarantee that a franchise will be renewed it is necessary to take out insurance policies in the shape of investment other than in television. If we look at the five major network companies which dominate the ITV network by virtue of their wealth and resources, we find that they have the following interests outside the television industry:

Thames Television owns a film company and has an interest in data bank computing services;

Granada has interests in television rentals, in bingo halls, in motorway services, in publishing (paperbacks like Panther, Paladin and Mayflower and the firm of Hart-Davis), in music publishing, cinemas and property;

London Weekend Television has interests in publishing (the large firms of Hutchinson and Constable), in travel, in property and in electronic equipment;

Associated Television, whose parent company is the powerful Associated Communications Corporation (ACC) has interests in feature films, theatres, cinemas, music publishers, Pye records, Ansofone and property;

Yorkshire Television, whose parent company is Trident Television - it also owns Tyne Tees Television - has interests in the Windsor safari park, in Scarborough Zoo, in commercial radio, in feature films and in property.

Other interconnections arise from the fact that commercial television is itself an attractive investment. Thus, Trafalgar House, which - among other interests - owns the *Daily Express* paper group, has a large holding in ATV. Telefusion, the television rental group, owns 15 per cent of the voting shares in Yorkshire Television. News International, which owns the *Sun* newspaper and the *News of the World*, has a large interest in LWT as do the *Daily Telegraph*, *The Observer*, Pearl Assurance, a merchant bank and a property developer. In Southern Television, one of the most profitable of the regional companies, more than a third of the voting shares are owned by Associated Newspapers (the *Daily Mail* group which pulled out of television in the early days of ITV and is now making up for its earlier failure of nerve) and another third by the Rank organisation, which is a multinational group with interests in cinemas, film, hotels, photocopying machines and the manufacture of television sets. A further 25 per cent is in the hands of D.C. Thomson, the Dundee firm which owns the right-wing *Dundee Advertiser*, publishes *Beano* and other comics, and is notorious for its opposition to any kind of union activity. The extensive participation of newspaper interests in commercial television is noticeable. This was a defensive measure on the part of the press which decided to become, where possible, a partner of its main competitor for advertising revenue and thus to soften the blow of competition. Indeed press investment is so conspicuous that the Television Act of 1964 contained a clause allowing the IBA or the Postmaster General (who was then the minister responsible for broadcasting) to suspend the contract of any programme company in which newspapers' holdings were 'leading to results contrary to the public interest.'

As we have seen in the case of Yorkshire Television, some of the ITV companies are themselves subsidiaries of larger undertakings. Granada is a subsidiary of the Granada Group of companies. Thames Television is jointly owned by EMI, which is not only one of the largest corporations in the country with interests in electronics, the film industry, sports industries, but is also the world's largest record company, and by British Electric Traction, which owes its name to the fact that it once owned the tramways in Buenos Aires but was more recently known for its ownership of the defunct Rediffusion Television company along with a string of launderettes - both of which it ran on much the same lines. It now controls a huge radio rental group, the Argus Press group publishing local weekly newspapers, a film distribution company and the Wembley Stadium.

Such complicated networks of business and financial interests are the natural outcome of the concentration of power in larger and larger undertakings as capital strives to increase or maintain its level of profits. On another level, however, those interests are reflected in a network of relationships which extend far beyond the limits of the television industry. Some of the directors of companies outside television but connected with it are likely to be on the list of 'the great and the good' from which members of the Boards of both the BBC and the IBA are drawn. Thus links can be and are formed which embrace both ITV and public service broadcasting. Members of the Boards of Governors may - 'wearing another hat', as they like to say - sit on the board of a company with interests in commercial television. As men and women who represent real and important capitalist interests they are not likely to look with favour on television programmes on either network which criticise these interests or their concepts of society, of 'law and order'. A series of programmes originated by Thames Television which was critical of certain aspects of how the medium is used had objections raised to it by a member of the board of Southern Television who represented external interests - objections which were sustained by the IBA so that when the series was repeated it was considerably truncated. What we must assume is that in conversations before or after board meetings or at social occasions the same sort of exchanges take place as occur in the television studios between television executives and politicians and other men and women of importance in our society - that opinions are canvassed, complaints noted, suggestions offered and received; in short, that they are among the multiple exchanges which go to shape the views of the managers of the commercial television companies. Clearly, too, such meetings provide opportunities at both a formal and informal level to enter into business relations, to seek help and advice, to explore ways of extending markets for equipment, for advertising and for programmes. It is not surprising that under a Tory government such interests should find their position strengthened and their grip on broadcasting extended.

8 The Market

Like any other industry the television industry requires a market. The electronic factories of the BBC or of the ITV companies produce commodities in the shape of programmes. These commodities are saleable. In the case of the ITV companies they are sold to other members of the commercial television network in Britain; but such sales are governed by rules formulated by the Authority which lay down that no profit may be made from the transaction. The system works in this way: major contractors - in other words the Big Five or network contractors - exchange programmes between themselves; regional contractors pay for their acquisitions according to a formula based on their NARAL (this is an important concept in commercial television) - that is to say, their net advertising revenue after the Levy has been deducted. The total effect of these transactions is that the producing companies can expect to cover direct costs, which do not include such items as staff wages, use of equipment, lighting, heating etc., but which do include payments to artists, the cost of materials such as film and videotape, copyright payments, payments to writers and so on, and expect to have a slight contribution to their overheads. But television programmes are also for sale abroad. This is a market which interests not only the commercial companies of ITV but also the BBC, whose selling (and buying) department, BBC Enterprises, has recently been formed into a commercial company.

Before the goods in the shape of television programmes can be sold they have to be packaged. Packaging is an important element in the production of all television programmes, whether for domestic consumption or for export. Thus, on air, one form of packaging is the style and the framework within which the programmes are presented on the screen. Station announcers who discharge this function are good-looking young men or women, who are in fact sales-people of the air. Packaging is to be seen in the elaborate electronically produced title-sequences and in the art work which sets the tone of the programme. Music plays its part in packaging. Baroque music, for example, is the ribbon commonly used to tie up cultural offerings on sculpture, music or art. Another form of packaging is the employment of presenters who lend their reputation and presence as a guarantee for the quality of the material about to be screened. Even when their physical presence is unnecessary or contrived they appear in picture to lend the stamp of their knowledge or charisma or both. Thus in the BBC series on civilisation Lord Clark (of Civilisation) emerged from behind Doric pillars or Gothic monuments to provide a brand image; David Attenborough floated through the waters of the Great Barrier Reef to give authority to statements about sea-life; in the United States and Canada Alastair Cooke with his mid-Atlantic accent fronts commodities bought from the British industry like *I Claudius* or *Upstairs Downstairs*, explaining, in the first case, that certain scenes had been judged too licentious for the American public to see. Packaging includes the tailoring of programmes to particular lengths - in the case of commercial television not longer than 57 minutes to allow time for commercials and the structuring of programmes so that they may be divided by 'natural breaks' to accommodate them. Breaks normally occur twenty minutes and forty minutes into the programme. This presents a problem to the film-makers or scriptwriters in that they must ensure that the viewers' interest is held over the intervening commercials so that there is no temptation to switch to another channel. The attempt to achieve this continuity of interest imposes a particular shape on programmes for commercial television. If the action of a play or the development of the argument in a documentary made for commercial television were charted linearily it would have a peak just before the twentieth minute and another before the fortieth with a third and final peak in its normal dramatic position just before the end of the programme. (In American programmes where the interruptions come thick and fast the gap for the commercials can be spotted by a recurring shot e.g. of a police headquarters, of the New York skyline, of a law court, of an oil-millionaire's ranch.) BBC programmes, simply because they do not have to accommodate commercials, have a different profile, which is likely to be the classical dramatic one of a build up of interest or excitement to a climax followed by some sort of resolution. These commodities are not only packaged; they come in various brands - lines which the producing organisations know will sell well. Thus the BBC is strong in costume drama, in travel and natural history; the programme contractors of ITV have their own brand products which include light entertainment shows, feature films made for television, drama series and even works by Shakespeare or Chekhov, provided always that the cast contains some saleable name, some theatrical knight or lady.

The aim in selling programmes abroad is naturally to penetrate the major markets which, in the case of British television organisations mean the United States, the Commonwealth and ex-colonial territories, and thereby to cover production costs and other costs such as dubbing into foreign languages or subtitling. After a certain point any sale is almost pure profit. One of the most difficult markets to penetrate was the American one. For years the American networks resisted British programmes on a variety of grounds, which included the view that the language used was incomprehensible, that the treatment of sex was unsuitable for American television, that the programmes were too high-brow, that the television series offered were too short - a mere six or seven programmes. (American television has carried industrial production further than it has gone in Britain by using teams of writers to deliver scripts for series that can last a year or more; significantly and honestly programmes are referred to as 'the product'.) The importance of the networks to British sales staff is that they can guarantee a coast-to-coast distribution and a correspondingly high price. The less profitable alternative is syndication to individual stations or to minor networks; of the latter the most important for sales has become PBS, the Public Broadcasting System, set up by the Nixon government with a federal government grant. It is not a wealthy network and depends for its finances on grants, subscriptions, advertising and sponsorships; it does not have the resources for large-scale dramatic productions and has therefore become a good customer for British programmes - so much so that its initials are said to stand for the Primarily British Service. These include both BBC productions like *Anna Karenina* and LWT's *Upstairs Downstairs*. Among the commercial companies ATV was among the first to make a determined effort to break into the American market, creating entertainment programmes which had a 'mid-Atlantic' tone and could - it was hoped - be shown in Britain and America with equal success. The mid-Atlantic solution tended to produce programmes which were slick but undistinguished and not very popular with British viewers. The

BBC, as it faced growing problems because the licence fee was lagging behind the rate of inflation, also began to embark on mid-Atlantic productions. These took the form of co-productions of which a notable and notorious example was *The British Empire* series, produced jointly with *Time-Life* and bearing all the marks of unhappy editorial compromise. (One of the problems was that the American view of early colonialism differs from the British one). Co-productions with American or European television and film organisations have become increasingly important as the BBC's financial position has deteriorated. Cases are quoted of producers who on proposing a project have been told that it will be considered provided they can provide co-production funds from some source here or abroad. It is a tactic in which the BBC trades its prestige and technical knowledge for financial support; clearly the policy raises questions about editorial control, choice of topics, and of style.

There is now a world market for television programmes for almost every country now has a television service of some kind although the distribution of sets is naturally very uneven. Thus in North America there are 2 persons per set, in Europe 4, in Latin America 12, in the Arab countries 40 and in Africa 500. Competition is fierce and the presence of the American networks and American production companies felt everywhere. Britain is fortunate in that as a highly developed industrial country it has the resources to make most of its own television programmes - as do other West European countries. Moreover the percentage of foreign material, which includes not only American programmes but Commonwealth and other material, is limited by the IBA to a figure of 14 per cent. This restriction was necessary because it is clearly cheaper to buy material already produced than to manufacture it oneself - a fact which tempted the programme contractors in the first euphoric years to buy indiscriminately in the American market. This policy is also resisted by ACTT, the film and television union, on the grounds that British crews, British technicians and British talent should be employed by British television; indeed the union campaigns actively against the amount of foreign, i.e. American, material to be seen on our screens. The BBC, in a self-denying ordinance, similar to its self-imposed restrictions on violence and material contrary to the public good, maintains a similar quota of foreign material. But while the BBC and the ITV companies buy relatively little, like the American networks they also sell programmes on a large scale throughout the world. The BBC sells up to 7,000 hours of programmes to 90 countries. The ITV yearbook is less explicit and merely states that 'almost every country in the world with a television system now buys ITV programmes'. 'One indication of ITV's prestige', it goes on, 'is that some overseas companies now buy programmes without having seen them.' Most television companies in ITV run major international selling operations which are accompanied by all the usual devices of high pressure selling, for example, sales fairs, 'usually held in hotels or other similar venues'; the annual television fair in Cannes is one of the best attended and most important. The BBC, it has to be added, is as fully involved in these selling operations as any of the programme contractors and uses precisely the same selling tactics. These efforts produce some surprising results such as the sale to Sweden, Norway and Yugoslavia of Ulster Television's *When Irish Eyes are Smiling*. But the question of precisely which programme is bought by any one television organisation is less interesting and certainly less important than the fact that the overwhelming bulk of the product sold is entertainment. Even more significant is that the market is dominated by the United States and Britain and that many countries are almost totally dependent on them for the bulk of the programmes transmitted in their territories. This dependence on foreign material is partly the result of lack of money and resources in these client states, which cannot afford to divert funds to build television studios or to finance programme-making; partly it is due to the fact that dependency has been fostered. In the sixties, when there was a considerable expansion of television in Asia, Africa and the Middle East, it was common practice for an American network to volunteer to help with the construction of a television station, providing the equipment on favourable terms, advising on facilities and layout, and to do so in such a way that the local station were technically unable to produce more than local news and chat shows. Thus they had small electronic studios which could not, except with great difficulty, produce drama of any kind. They were, however, equipped with telecine and videotape suites which allowed them to broadcast material on film or tape purchased abroad. This material was provided by the helpful network which offered a wide choice of entertainment in its programme catalogues. However, purchases from the catalogue were often conditional purchases; thus a well known and successful series would be offered as a package along with another series which had been a failure on the American network. Even countries as highly subsidised by the United States as Israel, and highly advanced in many respects (chiefly military), found that its television service was reliant on CBS, the American network, for much of its programming.

The mechanisms of the market in television programmes has created what has been described as a 'one-way flow' of material. This means that while material from the West accounts for 10 per cent of screen time in Eastern Europe, imports from Eastern European countries account for only two per cent of the screen time of the West European television organisations. The one-way flow covers the whole world; in most cases, along with the programmes go advertisements, all commercially produced material having slots already provided into which they can be dropped. 'The various undeveloped countries are having to permit commercials because they can't afford a television system otherwise,' is how a Vice President of *Time-Life* put it. A high-ranking executive of one giant American advertising agency explained the opportunity for the exploitation of television in these terms: 'I think the time is now, if it hasn't been already, to consider selling your product anywhere. With sub-titles, when you've a good television campaign or selling idea and it works in one place ... then you don't have to test the market any more, you go right to global marketing immediately.' Thus television has become an important agent for the marketing of goods produced in the developed countries of the world in any country with a television service. The advantages of this to the manufacturers and to the advertising agencies is obvious. Economic penetration goes hand in hand with the provision of entertainment; brand images can be established even with an audience that finds it difficult to read. To the question of how growth rates can be maintained and profits held up against their tendency to fall, the answer for American, Japanese and British firms is to move into overseas markets. Television programmes are their vanguards. They serve a dual purpose: they create in politically and economically dependent countries a concept of a life style that can - if only in part, only symbolically - be captured by purchasing the products advertised on the screen and they inculcate by constant exposure a western view of the world, of society and of human relationships.

Programmes are not, however, the only commodity for sale in the television world market. The other commodity is news. There are three main news agencies for the supply of television newsfilm. One of these is British. It is Visnews, which was set up jointly by Reuters News Agency, which already had a worldwide network of correspondents, the BBC, the Canadian Broadcasting Corporation and the Australian Broadcasting Commission - all three public service organisations. Another is UPI-ITN, a joint venture by the American news agency United Press International and Independent Television News, the news organisation which provides newscasts for the ITV network. The third is wholly American. It is CBS Newsfilm, the news gathering department of the Columbia Broadcasting System, which runs one of the three main American networks. There is a fourth, German news film agency - a fact which points to the importance, strength and wealth of the Federal German Republic and its position as the main ally of the United States in Western Europe. The three main agencies have a network of camera crews and reporters spread over most of the world, or at least those parts considered interesting and this excludes much of the Third World. At one time their material had to be flown back to a distribution point, which in the case of all three is and was London. Some of it still arrives by air but increasingly it is flown to the nearest satellite ground station and transmitted to London or elsewhere by satellite. In London it is edited and distributed to subscribers by cable, satellite or plane. The distribution is a huge, expensive and profitable business. It is also politically important. The dominance of the newsfilm agencies by America and Britain means, effectively, that on most television screens in the world - outside the Soviet Union and its eastern bloc neighbours, although they too receive film from the same sources - the view of world news projected is that of what we might call the Anglo-American consensus. Because, in spite of minor disagreements and rivalries, these two powers share certain basic views of the world situation. This means that the news is selected and edited from the point of view of western democracy, according to critieria which defines from a western point of view what constitutes a 'struggle for independence', what is 'important' and 'interesting'. To put in another way television news as supplied to most Third World and politically and economically dependent countries is compiled from material supplied by agencies which are incapable of looking at the world from the political perspective of the bulk of their consumers. It is naturally possible for the agencies' customers to change the text which accompanies the images on the newsfilm and thus to reinterpret what is seen on the screen. Presumably this is what will happen in the case of China, which has concluded an agreement for the supply of newsfilm with UPI-ITN. What it is not possible to do, however, is to supply material which is not filmed, which was judged not to be 'interesting' or 'important' by reporters and camera crews in the field who were persuaded that it would be rejected by their editorial bosses. Television newsfilm, for this reason, presents a view of the world that is based on the assumptions of the capitalist west, on that shared view of the world and of society which is called 'news sense'. News sense is sometimes described by journalists in television and elsewhere as if it were some faculty with which they and their colleagues are endowed. If asked to define it they will point to the similarity of judgements made by professionals in other news organisations. The fact that the UPI-ITN and Visnews will, on the same day, both consider the same stories important is a demonstration, they say, of news sense; as is the fact that BBC and ITN news will normally have the same stories in the same order. This is a circular argument which explains nothing. Shared judgements are not to be traced back to some mystical faculty but to the fact that the news professionals share the same views of society, respect the same taboos, have similar ideas about the importance or relevance to the viewer of social, economic and political events. Within individual countries this shared news sense is an important element in sustaining and reproducing the social order unchanged; in the international field it works within a view of the world based on the assumptions of the capital and neo-colonial west.

The ideology which has been evolved to justify the dominance of the Anglo-American news services is the concept of 'free flow of information', which is the application to the media of the concept of the free market. It is not a concept that has gone unchallenged by, for instance, the developing countries, which means in general former colonial territories and a number of non-aligned countries. They are beginning to demand 'a new international information order' - demands made in the knowledge that new technology now allows the use of satellites by great powers for the transmission of programmes directly to any spot on the globe. This move was the counterpart in the field of communications of the action taken by the OPEC countries to show that there are economic ways of challenging the hegemony of the developed countries. It was in the same spirit that the developing countries forced through two important meetings of the World Administrative Radio Congress (WARC), which allots radio, television and satellite frequencies, motions denying unused satellite frequencies to powers like the

United States which strongly advocated the right to have free use of any available frequencies. The developing countries - with very few exceptions - are unable to have their own satellites and are unlikely to have them for the next twenty years but they are determined not to give the powerful states which dominate the media squatters' rights. As one analyst of media politics puts it, they are 'demanding a moratorium on an international plane which could at the turn of the century result in cheap world communication when satellites become more easily available to all'. In other words, until such time as cheap communications are universally available, the developing countries are not prepared to allow the great powers to exercise rights which it might prove difficult to challenge or to occupy frequencies from which it might be difficult to dislodge them and which they would exploit to propagate their own ideologies, their own skewed view of politics, society and progress.

Such moves have been countered by the United States at various international conferences by a campaign for 'freedom of information' and by gestures of technical help to what Carter had called 'the newly influential countries' - the countries whose friendship and cooperation was needed in a common effort 'as the structure of world power changes'. What these newly influential countries want, however, is to be able to say that they do not wish to receive certain kinds of news, that they wish to gather and transmit their own view of the world and to escape 'from a dependence upon colonial legacies which have resulted in imbalances in communication structures and information flows'. 'People and individuals have the right to acquire an objective picture of reality by means of accurate and comprehensive information through a diversity of sources and means of information as well as to express themselves through various means of culture and communication'. So ran the declaration adopted at an intergovernmental conference to consider communications in Asia and the Pacific. It is not without its problems. What is meant, for instance, by 'an objective picture of reality'? But it conveys the feeling of governments and societies which have for many years been unable to learn about 'reality' in television terms from any except the Western newsfilm agencies and Western programme-selling agencies. Nationally and internationally the role of the broadcast media is a political question and will be settled politically.

9 New Technology I

Television, like many other industries, stands on the brink of important technological developments; some of them will modify the techniques employed in the electronic factories for the production of programmes - indeed have already begun to do so - while others may conceivably alter the nature of the medium itself. Among the first category is the change-over from film to videotape, which has been taking place for some years, but which new technology will speed up. One of the principal reasons for the switch is the fact that film uses a light-sensitive silver salt. Silver is becoming a scarce metal, the value of which has increased immensely because bullion speculators have been using it as a hedge against inflation; the price of the metal and of film has risen accordingly. Videotape which records images on a magnetic tape with a ferrous base is very much cheaper than film and has for many years been used alongside it. Initially, however, tape was at a disadvantage because it was more difficult to edit than film, which can easily be cut and joined. Cutting videotape damaged it and shortened its life; the process was also less precise than film-editing in which fine edits - down to a single frame - can be made manually. Tape eventually came to be edited electronically by using the video-recorders; the images on the tape were played by one machine on to a tape running on the other. When an edit had to be made the second machine was stopped where the cut began and started up again at the end of the edit. But there were still difficulties. The fact that two machines were tied up for a considerable time was unpopular with managements; but with the proliferation of machines in tape-suites and the development of techniques, which made the point for the edit easier to find, the editing of tape became routine. Now the use of computers has speeded up the process and made it more flexible.

Television cameras, which could record on tape, were cumbersome, however, so that the use of tape was for long confined almost entirely to recordings made in television studios or from fixed positions on outside broadcasts. Various ingenious attempts were made to adapt heavyweight equipment for making fiction and entertainment programmes on location, where normally only film would be used. Although these attempts were fairly successful it was apparent that real progress would come only with the development of reliable lightweight electronic cameras, the manufacture of which would depend on the use of miniaturisation to reduce both bulk and weight. When they appeared, these cameras gave rise to a wave of euphoria among groups of communicators outside the television industry who thought that lightweight portable gear - the portapak - was a weapon that might destroy the dominance of the television institutions, make possible an alternative form of television and allow them to mount an attack on the ideology of the medium, on the way in which it is conventionally used and on the assumptions about communications and society which underlie its operational techniques. What became apparent, however, was that the lightweight cameras were both temperamental and fragile and that for proper and continued operation they required - being pieces of high-grade technology - high-grade technical back-up services, which were too often not available to users. Thus the initial and somewhat naive hopes of an electronic revolution were blunted by the difficulty of remaining operational. Meanwhile at the institutional level the new cameras continued to be used and tested. Viewers began to catch sight of them in shot at sports events like the Olympic Games and it was as an adjunct to the recording of news events that they were first used. The new equipment came to be known for this reason, as ENG - electronic newsgathering equipment. The American television networks led the way in using ENG cameras for newsgathering to the point where the CBS station in Washington, for example, has ceased to use film at all for the purpose. News pictures from ENG cameras are either recorded on the spot on tape recorders or beamed back to the news studio for recording and editing. Meantime the dependability of the lightweight camera has increased to the point where it is widely used by producers and stations in the United States to make documentaries which would otherwise have been filmed; the same process is discernible in Europe.

Such developments have raised problems for the film and television unions. On the one hand, the probable eclipse of film as a recording medium threatens the livelihood of workers in film-processsing laboratories; on the other, the new lightweight electronic cameras mean that camera crews can be smaller. The jobs of film editors are also threatened. It is possible to argue in a reassuring way that the advent of any new technology may indeed mean that jobs have to be redistributed but that a decrease of employment in one area may well be offset by an increase in another. The new developments are taking place, however, at a moment when unemployment is rising - in Britain as part of a deliberate policy of the government which links the rise of unemployment with the decrease of inflation - the unions have therefore with every justification resisted the introduction of the new equipment except on their own terms. The point is not that the trade unionists are necessarily 'Luddite', although there is a natural reluctance to abandon old skills and a conservative tendency to decry the new medium of tape as less satisfactory than film which 'you can get your hands on'. What they feel is that, in a society where there is no provision for planned retraining and redeployment of members whose livelihoods are threatened by technological change, such change must be carefully controlled and new, additional skills be rewarded in terms of better wages. The unions may find more difficult to face the fact that, like the still camera, the electronic camera will in time become widely diffused in society and that the making of electronic pictures will cease to be the prerogative of professionals. Moreover, some at least of these amateur pictures will be of broadcast standard.

More spectacular than the introduction of ENG has been the development of satellites to transmit moving pictures from one part of the globe to another - a development closely linked to advances in rocketry for military purposes, to great power espionage from outer space, and to prestige operations like the landing of the first men on the moon. Such developments have led in the United States to close links between the Radio Corporation of America and its television network, NBC, and the Pentagon, which is one of the great centres of the United States military-industrial complex. The economic and military power of the United States has ensured that, so far as the Western powers are concerned, American interests, are paramount in the international consortia set up to fund and control the satellites which today bring pictures onto our screens so regularly that their arrival there is no longer worthy of comment. The first satellites orbited round the earth rising and setting and therefore could transmit to their targets only when they rose above the horizon; now satellites are more likely to be geo-stationary - that is to say, stationed some 23 thousand miles out in space at a constant altitude and keeping pace with the revolutions of the earth. The effect is that they remain stationary above one spot unless they are deliberately moved, which happened, for instance, with a satellite first located over the Rocky Mountains to transmit schools programmes and later moved to a position over India to transmit instructional programmes to community antennas. The pattern of transmission is generally that signals from ground stations are beamed to geo-stationary satellites and reflected by them to receiving stations, which then relay them by cable to the television organisations for recording or transmission.

The advantages of satellite transmission are obvious if we recollect that the range of a television transmitter mast is limited to the line of sight from the top of the mast. For this reason the British television system requires a network of around 2300 transmitters, some linked by cables, others by 'dishes' - the large antennas which are used for short-wave communications - to obtain almost complete coverage of the country. In general, the signal is carried from the point of origin to the transmitters by expensive co-axial cables, which have to be laid over long distances. Had satellites been available for transmission purposes in the immediate post-war years there is no doubt that they would have been used to link transmitting and receiving stations and to do so more cheaply than the cable network. Today in the United States, for instance, the three great networks rely on cable to link their stations to their affiliates through the Union; independent stations of the Public Broadcasting Service, however, can be linked by satellite at far lower cost. Satellites are an obvious way to overcome some of the problems set by geography. In Norway, for instance, transmitters are in some cases required on each side of a narrow fjord in order to get a signal to homes at sea level; Switzerland faces problems of the same nature in its mountain valleys. Frequencies have already been allocated to all European countries which will allow satellites to broadcast signals to their national territories, thus solving the problem of reaching difficult areas. The problem is that there is bound to be overspill beyond national borders; this might be relatively unimportant where programmes are concerned but becomes a threat when it is a question of commercials. Thus

Luxembourg, which in the thirties led the way in commercial radio, has been allocated satellite frequencies for coverage which clearly will not be limited to the tiny area of the Duchy in which important transnational business and commercial interests are based. Its programmes and its commercials are bound to be available in Germany, Belgium and France; Luxembourg has, however, undertaken not to broadcast in English. The advantages of satellites for television coverage in the Indian sub-continent, in Latin America, in Canada and the Soviet Union (which has long practice in their use for this purpose), for Africa and the Pacific area are obvious but only rich countries can afford them.

So long as the programmes are locally originated, reflected up to a satellite and then passed on to a local ground station, there are no major political problems. Difficulties arise when discussion turns to the possibility of broadcasting from satellites not to an intermediary ground station but directly to viewers' homes. This is already technically possible; the only equipment required by the viewer is a dish-shaped antenna some 60 centimetres in diameter and an adaptor between the antenna and the set. But what is to prevent 'the free flow of information' from taking the form of political propaganda by the great powers directed at individual homes, thus beginning a television war comparable to the radio propaganda exchanges which have been going on since the end of the Second World War between the Western Powers and the Soviet Union. It is true that there are agreements covering the use of satellite frequencies but experience with radio shows that the great powers are ready to break any agreement if it is to their advantage. Satellite communications are a focus for political and commercial rivalries in which the prizes are immense. The struggle for ascendancy will be correspondingly bitter.

Not all developments in television technology are of such global importance. At a more prosaic level there is the development of the ability to transmit information to subscribers for reception on a domestic television receiver. In Britain both the BBC and the IBA have developed services of this nature. The Post Office engineers have produced their own version which allows a subscriber to ring up for information, which is then displayed on a screen. The market for such apparatus is still small, but there is undoubtedly a demand for it in business circles where subscribers want to have immediate access to stock exchange quotations or to the movement of the metal market rather than waiting for a tape service. What is more doubtful is the degree to which domestic viewers will avail themselves of the services offered. At this level the impetus for such immediate access to data depends on the extent to which work becomes decentralised with researchers and office-workers carrying out their tasks at home rather than in an office and on the urgency with which viewers feel the need to know *now* what is happening in the world rather than waiting for a couple of hours till the next newscast. The appetite for instant absorption of news has been carefully cultivated by the broadcast media - chiefly by radio with its news headlines at regular intervals or its continuous, rolling news broadcasts like those of LBC. There is a real sense in which the consumption of news has gone hand in hand with the consumption of commodities; it is part of the drive for customers on the part of the broadcasting institutions, which have managed to convince the public that the concept of being first with the news is a social virtue instead of merely a professional convention. Beyond that, the visionaries of technology look forward to the time when we shall have our daily papers delivered electronically and reproduced in our own homes. What is not usually spelt out is that we should have to bear the cost of the paper on which the news is reproduced ourselves. We shall, they say, have access not only to data banks but to libraries of videotapes and taped films. We shall watch television on screens as large as our living room walls. We shall play video games. We shall receive a multiplicity of television signals carried by laser beams through thin plastic tubing. What is less frequently discussed is in what ways the material in this video utopia will be restricted. A data bank can provide only such information as has been put into it; in our society that information is not likely to include the subversive, the radical, the unorthodox. The function of 'gate-keeping' will again be at work here. Experience with the data services available today shows that, not unexpectedly, the news and information provided by them is determined by the ideology of our capitalist society.

It is not perhaps surprising that two of the most highly developed attempts to supply the services of the latest media technology are to be found in Japan. In the 'model community' of Higashi-Ikoma near the city of Osaka - a community composed of upper-class households with above average incomes - a number of households were provided (without charge) with the following services: nine channels carrying normal television programmes but with high quality reception and 14 other channels providing local programmes and information services - of these one channel provides studio productions (general news, education, information of various kinds); seven provide request programmes on payment; three provide programmes which repeat constantly. Other channels provide stills and captions dealing with weather, timetables, medical information and 'useful addresses and telephone numbers'. Personal news can also be exchanged. The system can also be linked to a videotelephone. What is interesting is not so much the varied services offered as that the enterprise is looked on by the electronics manufacturers as a laboratory experiment. It is paralleled by another experiment in Tama Newtown, where the families are described as lower middle class living in small houses. They had the opportunity to receive a facsimile machine to print out a newspaper, a 'flash information service' of recent news, a service which produces recent news in the form of a memo, and a 'miniature-TV service', whereby important news can be displayed in a corner of the screen while another programme is running. What is cheering about these experiments is that although the apparatus was installed free and cost nothing to use only half the families approached agreed to accept it, and that in Higashi-Ikoma audience research produced the following answers to the question whether the viewers found the service useful: Very useful - 8.9 per cent; Fairly useful - 54 per cent; Hardly any use - 31.4 per cent; Useless - 5.7 per cent. This was interpreted by the authorities as meaning that the majority i.e. over 62 per cent of the users considered the experiment useful. Another reading would be that 85 per cent of the users were lukewarm, to say the least, in their reactions.

Some of the prophets of media technology are obviously falling into the trap of technological determinism - the view that if something is technically possible it is both desirable and bound to be realised in practice. There is a good deal of evidence, however, to show that societies do not adopt technological change in this deterministic way. Factors influencing decisions to develop a particular technology are, in the case of capitalist enterprises, the probability of profit and the existence of a potential market; in the case of the capitalist state the determining factors are likely to be political or military. Once a technological innovation like television has been established, however, and the existence of a mass market is demonstrated, then there is a strong incentive for manufacturers to push for technological developments. In Britain, for instance, the cycle of renewal for television sets is assumed to be in the region of ten years; in that period all set owners will have acquired a new set. In order to ensure that such a renewal cycle functions the manufacturers have regularly come up with compelling reasons why the public should acquire new equipment. First came the change from 405 to 625 line-standard sets; that was followed by the change to colour. Today the point of growth in the mind of the manufacturers is to be found in the sale of video-cassette recorders for the recording of programmes off-air or for the reproduction in the home of tapes of feature films or porn movies; the mass market has yet to be developed but it is a sign of growing (or at least stimulated) demand that recorders can now be hired in the same way as television receivers. Alongside the development of the cassette goes the search for the video-disc which will be played like a record either with a stylus or a laser; if the system can be standardised and the price of manufacture kept low enough the expectation is that a teen-age market for video-recordings of pop groups could be exploited. But the fact that a great recording company like Decca has been in financial trouble both in the United States and in Britain because the teen-age public finds it more difficult to buy records on the scale that it did a few years ago does not augur well for the video-disc.

Some of the complications attendant upon the development of new media technology are illustrated by the development of cable television in the United States. When it was first introduced various groups and individuals placed high hopes on the concept of 'the wired city' as a means of effecting a reform of the medium. If homes were linked by cable to a local station, it was argued, and if the United States Federal Communications Commission, which controls broadcasting even if in a somewhat lax way, were to abide by its ruling that two channels on any cable system had to be available for local programmes, then an alternative television service might be built up in a number of centres. There would be free access to anyone interested and the possibility of feed-back from viewers in their homes. But development was slow, in part because the provision of cables in large towns, where they would be most useful because the steel-frame buildings of American cities cause distortion to the pictures on viewers' screens, proved too costly. Developments in the provision of cables therefore took place in small and medium towns which - unlike the big cities - have normally access only to the two or three main networks and a local station as opposed to the

12 or 13 channels available in large centres. With the growth in cable networks went an increased interest in their exploitation by large financial interests; the result is that rich companies with very large turn-overs are engaged in providing programmes for cable subscribers. Thus Teleprompter has an annual turn-over of over 124 million dollars; other large concerns are deeply involved with the backing of firms already deeply committed to the electronics or media industries: General Electric; Time inc., the great magazine publishers; the *Los Angeles Times*, the very conservative West Coast paper; film production companies and so on. What is provided by the cable services is a long way from the local participatory programmes envisaged by the media reformers. Instead there are films (unbroken by commercials which on normal American television come up ruthlessly to interrupt the action, the opening sequences and even the credits at the end), sporting events, entertainment shows, children's programmes, educational programmes, 'black entertainment television', news and religion.

If between 1975 and 1980 the number of cable systems rose from 170 to 1,400 with some five million viewers, the reason is to be sought in the dissatisfaction in an important section of the audience with the programmes offered by the commercial companies. A recent audience research poll discovered that only 30 per cent of those interviewed expressed satisfaction with the networks; 67 per cent thought that the commercial companies did not have the interest of the viewers at heart. It was this dissatisfaction that the financial interests which provide the programmes for cable television services cashed in on. To do so they began using satellites to reach the cable distribution centres. Thus a Pay TV company called Home Box Office has been using an RCA Communications satellite (Satcom 1) for the last five years to get national coverage for films. The cost of hiring the satellite varies (according to use) from about half a million to over one million dollars per annum; but satellites give national coverage and satellite ground stations are relatively cheap to build - as little as 12,000 dollars, which is considerably less than a microwave relay station with a range of only some 25 miles and a cost of 60,000 dollars. In 1983 there will be direct transmission by satellite into viewers' homes at a charge of 15 dollars a month per subscriber. Sears Roebuck, the great trading house whose illustrated catalogues found their way into thousands of homes has expressed interest in the satellite for commercial television programmes bearing its name. What will they be? Films, sporting events, musicals.

The process is a familiar one. What began as a local initiative with, in some cases, an idealistic belief in the possibility of providing a different kind of television, has fallen into the hands of large concerns with large capital sums for investment in programmes and equipment and to launch new satellite services. But these services cost money. A subscription to Pay TV can cost as much as 500 dollars a year - a considerable sum for many Americans. Those who cannot afford the various subscriptions will have to remain content with the offerings of the networks. In effect the American viewing public shows every sign of becoming divided into those who can afford relatively good uninterrupted programmes and those who must make do with second best. The free play of the market forces, in short, produces its usual results. In the meantime the ruling that cable services must restore two channels for local programming has been successfully challenged in the courts.

In a more rational society - in a socialist society - other considerations would govern the development of mass communications technology. These would include a questioning of the priority to be assigned to mass communications as opposed to medical research, to education, to the development of alternative sources of power, to the fight against poverty and the provision of housing and services to large masses of deprived men and women throughout the world. Beside such goals the concept, for instance, of a 'space post office', which is feasible and which would allow the transmission of letters in the form of signals to and from satellites - the technology is already there - would enjoy a very low priority.

In the meantime there are those who, within the limits of present-day technology, feel that developments are possible which have to do, not with the elaboration of hardware, but with the manner in which that hardware is used. It is not necessary to subscribe to the extravagant and fanciful views of Marshall McLuhan, who believes that communications systems are the main force for change in human society and who considerably distorts history to make his point, in order to feel that television, used in different ways from those we have become accustomed to, might play a different role in our society. Video, for example, could be developed as a means of providing information and propaganda for groups with similar aims - old age pensioners fighting for rights, tenants' groups, women's groups, political parties, pressure groups of one kind or another. The use of television at this level has been hampered, as we have seen by the difficulty of technical maintenance of equipment and by the unreliability of both cameras and recording machines. On a larger scale, there has been some development in Britain of community television, an idea embraced at one point by business interests who were willing to back pilot projects in order to see what market there was for a somewhat different product - pay TV, a system whereby viewers pay for what they choose to watch (usually old feature films or sport as in the United States) by putting money into a meter. The advocates of community television have more enlightened goals. They believe that broadcasts aimed at, and, as far as possible, made by members of a local community can stimulate interest in the community's affairs and encourage participation in decision making and in local politics. In Britain the experience of the five community stations which came into operation between 1972 and 1974 was not very encouraging, in spite of some admirable attempts to provide local news coverage which eschewed the institutional impartiality of the BBC and ITN. Some of the difficulties encountered were foreseeable and perhaps inevitable. One was that initiatives in suggesting programmes and in carrying them out tended to come from those members of the community who were already good communicators - that is to say, who had enjoyed certain levels of educational attainment; they were therefore not necessarily representative of the community as a whole. There were problems too about control of the stations which did not, for example, put into practice the idea put forward by the film and television union, ACTT, that the community should have the major say in electing representatives on the governing bodies or that the latter should be chosen by local groups: trades councils, churches, PTAs, women's groups etc.

The problem of community television has deeper roots, however. Many of the advocates of community television do not appear to have a very clear definition of what is meant by 'a community'. To what extent is it possible to call 'a community' the place where men and women sleep and spend their free time while working elsewhere. Perhaps the true community is to be found in the plants of British Leyland or of Ford's but in that case who would control the community or plant television service - the BL chairman or the shop stewards? Or suppose there had been community television at Corby, which is a community in the true sense of the word, would the steelworkers have been able to have access to it? Would they have taken it over and run it? Would it have been a rallying point for political argument and consciousness-raising? The fact is that 'community television' cannot be divorced from the political realities of the society in which it functions. For it to become a social force it would have to overcome the feeling, which has been inculcated by the educational system, that ordinary people have little possibility of governing their own choices, or taking decisions on matters in the public domain, in the community. Where they have learned to defend their interests and to promote them is precisely in the place of work - in factories, hospitals, offices, schools and workshops. But the right to employ television in such 'communities' would be a political one and presupposes a situation in which the trade unions had established certain rights within the plant. Political movements do not come from the media but they can use the media for their ends.

The questions arises whether, given the relative proliferation of television equipment, there is any possibility of developing some sort of alternative television broadcasting system. In Britain as things stand at present the possibilities are almost non-existent. The authorities have since 1926 had broadcasting under efficient control. In the United States, where controls are looser and there are a number of independent public stations, programmes appear from time to time on prison conditions, on social history and on social questions, which would find it difficult to reach the screen in Britain. The same is true for some European countries like Denmark and Holland. Then there is the case of Italy where several hundreds of television stations operate outside the state-controlled television networks. Some of these are purely business ventures exploiting the frequencies they have taken over in order to make a quick profit by commercial advertising. Others have specialised in pornography or striptease competitions for housewives. Some have been mouthpieces of the extreme right; others have represented the policies and interest of the left. (A Rome station run by a left-wing group was machine-gunned and set on fire when transmitting a programme by a women's group.) The reason for this state of affairs is political. The even balance of power between the block represented by the Catholic Christian Democrats on the one hand and the Communist Party on the other has led to what the Italians call a state of *immobilismo* - a situation in which political intervention from central government becomes difficult. The pirate television stations are exploiting something like a paralysis of the central power of the state which has caused a vacuum into which large business interests (publishers and newspapers) have moved with the result that promising local initiatives have been killed off. This brings us back to the essential point which must be kept in mind when discussing the use and development of television; it is that the constraints society lays on the use of any medium of communication are political and that, in order to change the way in which a medium like television is used, we first have to change society. In a talk on the function of radio given in 1930, Brecht had something to say which is as applicable today to television as it was then to radio: 'It is no task of ours (i.e. of the left) to renew ideological institutions by innovations on the basis of the present social system ... These proposals cannot be achieved in this social system - can be achieved in another.'

10 New Technology II

Like many other industries, television as we have seen is undergoing rapid technological changes. These are in part spin-offs from other areas: thus the use of satellites to transmit television signals is a by-product of super-power rivalries in outer space, as is the rapid advance in the miniaturisation of equipment and the use of computers. Others derive from the production needs of the electronic factories in which television programmes are manufactured: these include the ability to edit videotape (which is rapidly replacing film as a means of recording programmes and events) easily and accurately by the use of computers and the introduction of reliable lightweight electronic cameras for reporting and for use in studios. Others, such as the video-cassette, are the result of that constant search for profits which is the driving force of capitalism - one less concerned with social needs than with balance sheets. Another example is the video-disc which is only held back because of uncertainties about its chances in the markets of the world. Such technological changes are part of a wider movement of change and investment in change which will undoubtedly alter our social habits as consumers and viewers, but will not in any fundamental way affect the production relationships in our society: the relation between capital and labour, the way in which wealth is produced and profit distributed.

The microchip revolution is in this sense a limited one; developments in the electronic media are equally limited in their effects. The theory that because of the new media we inhabit an 'electronic village' - a view put forward by Marshall McLuhan, the intellectually dubious Catholic populist media guru of the sixties - is little more than a figure of speech. We may frequently receive the same signals and watch the same programmes but the way in which the signals are 'read' differs from place to place and from class to class. In this respect, it seems improbable that there is much in common between the 'readings' of a sweat-shop worker in the monetarists' model society, Hong Kong, and those of a viewer on the North American continent or in South-East England.

This is not to deny that developments in the mass media have affected social customs and the way in which we conduct and plan our lives. Thus the increase in the number of 'television families' in Britain in the fifties was accompanied by a sharp fall in cinema attendances with important effects on the British film industry. If there is a noticeable decline in the size of the television audience today it may in part be due to saturation with television; but the astonishing boom in the sale of video-cassettes is clearly an important contributory cause. Britain has the largest number of video-cassette recorders (VCRs) in proportion to its population size of any developed country. The buyers of these machines and of the cassettes that go with them are largely, so market researchers tell us, what they describe as C1s - that is to say, they fall into the income bracket which includes the skilled workers as well as members of the middle classes. In an era of uncertainty and inflation people earning good wages are investing in consumer hardware; in an era of unemployment workers who have been made redundant get rid of their modest redundancy payments in the same way because that tiny capital sum would otherwise make them ineligible for supplementary benefit.

What appears to be happening as a result of the arrival of the video-cassette is that around 10 per cent of the potential audience spends a considerable part of its viewing time doing one of two things. Either people watch programmes recorded off-air at times that suit them better than the transmission times (because for instance, of clashes between the various channels) or else they are watching programmes on cassettes which range from feature films to soft porn or (though this is less likely) programmes made specially for the cassette market. Among the latter are the 'Falklands' cassettes produced by BBC and ITN. This represents the first instance of news coverage being sold as a commodity.

One indication of the spread of the habit of viewing cassettes rather than direct transmissions is provided by teachers' reports of pupils who no longer watch 'the telly', but only cassettes or video-games. Press stories tell of school children saving up for porn cassettes to be played when their parents are out. On the positive side, the VCR has allowed a portion of the television audience to escape from the tyranny of the programme schedules. It is a development which, if it continues, will call into question the philosophy and practice of the programme-planners. This is based on the idea that 'channel loyalty' is all-important — that it is necessary to catch the audience at the beginning of the evening and to discourage viewers from switching to the competitors; hence the cross-announcements from BBC1 to BBC2 and from Channel 4 to ITV. The consequences of such alterations in viewing habits, together with the increase of programme sources (there will be more in the near future), are bound to include organisational changes in the broadcasting systems.

The electronics industry has traditionally required some new development at intervals of about ten years to maintain its profitability. (The parallel with the production of new car models is obvious; obsolescence is a prerequisite for both the motor car and the electronics industries.) Thus there was the change from a 405 lines system to the new standard of 625 lines, which effectively rendered almost all TV sets anachronistic; then followed the change-over from black and white to colour. It is significant that there has been no real attempt by the industry to improve the sound signal that accompanies the pictures on television. All that would be required is a small and cheap modification to receivers. However, such a change would not be profitable and has therefore not been adopted. The next important development was the sale for home use of VCRs. What is now imminent is the widespread use of cable for the distribution of television signals alongside and together with the introduction of DBS - direct broadcasting by satellite.

Cable has been used for the distribution of television and

radio signals in Britain for many years. Subscribers rent a set connected to a cable system which, using a central aerial system, provides them with a better signal, particularly in large cities where high buildings interfere with broadcast signals. Cable signal companies depend for their profitability on having a large number of subscribers in a compact, densely populated distribution area. Cable as a relay system is therefore not profitable outside the great conurbations and for that reason has not spread to the countryside. Even so, there are over 12 million rented sets in Britain linked to cable distribution services, which do not provide their own programmes but carry BBC and ITV material. Since the sixties there have, it is true, been a number of experiments in cable television such as that approved by the Labour government in 1966 for pay television - the basis of which is that the viewers pay to see programmes not otherwise available to them - to be introduced on a small scale in London and Sheffield. These experiments were unsuccessful, which means unprofitable. The exact reasons for their lack of success, which presumably include the fact that viewers could get as good or better programmes free, have never been disclosed. In the seventies there were further local ventures - notably in Greenwich, Bristol and Milton Keynes, where an attempt was made to link cable to what was rather vaguely described as community television. The use of the word 'community' raised a host of questions. There was a not unfounded suspicion in many people's minds that the companies involved were prepared to pay lip-service to the ideal of community programmes, provided they were inexpensive, but that their ultimate aim and main source of profit was to be some form of pay TV based on sports, feature films and other material available on the market, chiefly from the United States. (The production of television programmes is an extraordinarily costly business and has never been seriously considered by the advocates of pay TV.) When the Tory government came to power it granted licences to twelve cable sites for pay TV with a 2-year licence. Admittedly the licensees work under a number of restrictions covering the showing of films ('18' certificates only after 10 p.m.); no advertising or sponsorship; programme schedules to be submitted to the Broadcasting Department of the Home Office, which exercises a control and censorship function according to guidelines which are not publicly available. (The increasing responsibility for both pay TV and broadcasting in general by the department, which is also responsible for the police force and public order, is a disquietening development of recent years.)

This experiment is entirely in line with the Conservative policy of privatisation. As with previous pay TV experiments it is difficult to discover how successful (profitable) they have been. Once again there must be a suspicion that these ventures are in the nature of holding operations while the interests involved wait for other more favourable operational conditions - such as that they should not be required to carry BBC and ITV programmes or to be fettered by official controls over their output.

It was not until 1981 that the Tory government revealed its true intentions over cable. It first set up a Technology Advisory Panel with a membership drawn predominantly from the electronics industry. The panel was instructed to 'ensure that government policies and actions are securely based on a close appreciation of market needs and opportunities'. The accent on profitability was consonant with the political philosophy of the Thatcher government. This panel produced for the Tories a report on cable systems which discussed the development of a widespread cable system in terms of what it called 'powerful economic and industrial arguments' related to direct markets for equipment 'which could total £3,000 million or more' and to overseas sales of programme material, information services and expertise. There would also clearly be very large financial rewards to the cable industry for the manufacture and laying of the network. 'Not only,' it says, 'would there be the initial £2,000-£3,000 million of capital investment' but, with the sale of various decoders, 'an additional expenditure of £1,500 million' could be generated. They were therefore 'in no doubt that cable systems could be a source of much profitable commercial activity', particularly when seen in conjunction with the growing market for consumer and business electronics and the improved market prospects for direct broadcasting by satellite (DBS). At one point the report becomes curiously anxious. Referring to the possibility of an election at some date prior to May 1984, it urges that a decision on cable be taken promptly otherwise there is 'little prospect of a modern cable industry being established in the UK'. This uneasiness about the prospect of an election seems curious. The urgency is part of an attempt to persuade the government to invest in modern cable systems employing not the present copper cables, with their limited capacity for programmes, but the new fibre optic cables, capable of carrying several hundred signals simultaneously through fine glass tubing, which is cheaper to lay than present-day copper cabling. On the other hand, it reflects their anxiety that satellite broadcasting may be established before a cable network has been laid. References to the social implications of the introduction of cable, speculation as to the type of programmes that would be provided by narrowly commercial and socially uncontrolled commercial interests without production facilities of their own, and considerations of the effects of cable on the present broadcasting institutions are hurried and almost casual.

The report of the panel was referred by the government to a three-person committee chaired by Lord Hunt, who has no obvious expertise in the field. Its remit was not to discuss the implications of cable television and its social and economic effects, but rather to make a swift decision on how the technical recommendations could best be implemented. Admittedly the Home Secretary in his terms for setting up the Hunt Committee made a reference to the need to safeguard public service broadcasting - by which he meant the BBC *and* ITV. Nevertheless, it cannot be said that much serious attention was given to the problem in the course of the committee's deliberations, which lasted only a few months. Major decisions on the future of broadcasting have in the past - witness the Pilkington Committee Report of 1960 and the Annan Report of 1977 - taken a long time, during which large amounts of evidence are submitted and discussed by the committees.

What was crucially important was the stand the Hunt Committee would take on programming and what are usually called 'standards'. 'Standards' is an ambiguous word, packed full of ideological assumptions and preconceptions about the nature of society and of the function of the broadcasting media in society. Being a term which reflects the contradictions within a society it can be used either in a conservative and reactionary sense or in a sense which is critical of the values accepted by society and its broadcasting institutions. The committee showed where it stood on the matter by avoiding any serious discussion of the question of 'standards' and by taking the view that market forces should have free play. Thus, on the question of taste and decency (another term that conceals complex assumptions about society and about the viewers), it was content to recommend an authority which would 'keep in touch' with what was put on the air and take retrospective action. There was no question of making the cable operators provide community programmes - a duty which is laid on operators in Canada, for example. Instead, a vague hope was expressed that cable systems' 'relationship with a contribution to their local communities might become a source of mutual pride'.

The system envisaged by the committee is one in which the key figure is the cable operator - the manager of a local cable system 'who puts together a package of cable services to sell to customers from whom he collects revenue'. The cable operator will have an effective local monopoly; he will therefore have to acquire a franchise for the right to operate from an authority which will oversee performance. (The language of the committee's report throughout is patriarchal.) Programmes will be acquired from programme or service providers, who will be - but the committee does not mention this - pedlars of cheap American products and other material which has not been accepted by the present broadcasting institutions. There will be no limit on the number of programme channels the operator may provide; monitoring of the operators' programming will be 'reactive' but will not entail 'constant supervision of the services provided'. It is admitted, however, that there would have to be a body 'to keep in touch with what is going on', 'to keep an eye on the use of United Kingdom programme material and developments in advertising', 'to judge whether cable operators are living up to their promises' and 'to respond flexibly as cable develops'. This easygoing attitude with its reliance, in a curious passage dealing with the need to show '18' films for shift workers, on an electronic locking device to keep such material from the kiddies, is strikingly at variance with that taken to the proposal a couple of years earlier that Channel 4 should be freed from the supervision of the Independent Broadcasting Authority. That proposal was rejected as too liberal and open to abuse. Profits, it seems, are like money which, as the proverb has it, does not stink. The possible results of such a loosely controlled commercial system are obvious. (Canada's first pay TV service, to which subscriptions were slow, has signed up a $30 million deal with Playboy Enterprises for the production of soft porn films.) Cable operators with no production resources and no considerations except profitability will emulate the producers of material for the cassette market. The knock-on effect on the programming of the broadcasting institutions from commercialism of this kind would be far-reaching.

Clearly, cable in itself is neither better nor worse than any other technology. What matters is how a given technology is used and for what ends. The media utopians have been talking for years about 'the wired society' and 'cabling the nation'. They have described models of electronic households with reactive communications systems offering information and entertainment, access to electronic data-banks, shopping and banking by remote control; they have described the possibility of plebiscites, public opinion polls and even elections being conducted by the cable systems linking households to cable-operating centres. This utopia needs to be looked at carefully and with some suspicion for it could be the extension of privatisation to the social and political field - the erection of a perfect feedback system, an Orwellian vision of citizens feeding on the media and feeding back through the media the views on politics, on peace and war, on social questions which the media had provided in the first place. It is the logical extension of that pressure to remove public affairs from the arena of public debate - such as trade union and other meetings - and to return the moment of decision to the home. The philosophy is typified by Tory advocacy of postal ballots of trade unionists.

There are, however, other less frightening possibilities. Cable could, under certain circumstances, allow a multiplicity of voices to be heard on radio and television. Its development could lead to the kind of network of communications systems which Enzensberger envisaged in his seminal essay on the media industry - a network so extensive that it would be difficult for local or central controls to be exercised over it. (But what about bugging as with the present telephone system?) Short of such remote developments there could be an opportunity under certain political circumstances - for politics and economics are the determining factors in the elaboration of any communications system - of cable being used as a common carrier to which groups, trade unions, and other movements would have access with a freedom approximating to that enjoyed by publishing houses. Even with the limited network proposed by the Hunt Committee some such development would be possible. The committee realised this and presumably saw the dangers inherent in it - namely, that voices lying outside the broadcasting consensus, outside mainstream broadcasting, might get air-time. It therefore specifically excludes political parties and organisations, along with religious bodies, from direct participation in the ownership of any cable-operating companies. Even the relatively innocuous idea that the TUC or the Labour Party might have one of the many possible channels is therefore ruled out.

Under the present government there is not likely to be any

approximation to that freedom of communication which many on the left envisage as the goal of cable, a technology which could in theory free television from the restrictions of surveillance by government-appointed bodies and set free a multiplicity of radical voices. It has to be reiterated in this connection that such a realm of freedom is far off; that it would require for its achievement a fundamental change in the nature of society; and that, like all media operations, it would present the left with a problem which its supporters are often reluctant to face up to. The problem is that within the foreseeable future the number of channels will be limited by the amount of capital required in the same way as channel time is limited by considerations of money and staffing. From this follows the need for someone to exercise a gate-keeping function - that process of deciding what goes on the air, of deciding who has access, which is the concomitant of the limitations of time, and money and channels. Whether centrally or locally, decisions will have to be taken about access. The nature of such decisions can be crudely presented in the form of the questions: Should racists have access to cable channel time? Should sexist material be broadcast over cable networks? Should voices and images which perpetuate repressive systems be allowed? There is a liberal attitude which says that they must, and that the viewers should be allowed to make up their own minds. There is a radical point of view which, if it is honest, says that any socialist society would have to defend itself and deny access to such voices and such images.

Even if we draw back from visions of a socialist society defending itself against the voices of reaction and return to Britain of the eighties and nineties, the question of control still has to be faced. One obvious proposal (which would, one hopes, have the support of a Labour government) is that cable should not be privately owned but come under British Telecom which would operate the system as a common carrier and, as such, make it available in the same way as the telephone system is today. Time on the air would be available to those persons and institutions able to afford it. There are a large number of services which industry and business require for the transmission of information and data which could be catered for in this way together with such other devices as the monitoring of gas and electricity services, facsimile services, alarm systems on buildings and homes, even electronic shopping. There would also be, as the bulk of the usage, programme services. In either case, there should be some overall controlling authority responsible for the supervision of programme standards and for the encouragement of local and community services; it would also have the duty of ensuring that access was made available to groups and interests in our society which today find it difficult to obtain a hearing. (Within Dutch television, the controlling authority has the duty of ensuring that points of view not otherwise given air-time do have opportunities to be heard.) It would still be naive to think that the question of editorial control or laying down broad programme policies can be avoided. By whom should these powers be exercised and by whom should the ground rules be drawn up? Would it be too much to hope that under a Labour government (not to speak of a socialist government) a national cable authority might be set up which included among its members people other than the middle- and upper-class men and women who form the overwhelming majority on the boards of the BBC and the IBA and of the various advisory councils set up by these bodies? Too much to hope that interests at present unrepresented on them like the unions, the workers in the broadcasting and film industries, the black community, the women's movement, should have a say and an opportunity to decide policies?

Closely linked to the development of cable is the coming of DBS. Television signals have been sent from one part of the globe to another by satellite for more than twenty years, and the use of satellites to beam coverage into newscasts is now so routine that it does not merit special mention on our screens. Up to now satellites have been linked to elaborate ground stations, one of which transmits the signal (from Singapore, perhaps) to the satellite which then reflects it to another ground station like the main one in the United Kingdom, in Cornwall. With the introduction of DBS viewers will have their own ground stations, as it were, in the shape of a dish-shaped antenna on their roof or in their garden. Since the antenna is rather large, many people, particularly in towns, will rely on some central antenna, which might be on the roof of a block of flats, or even more remote and connected to the individual homes by cable. The system has been functioning for some time in the United States where subscribers - for a substantial fee - can receive signals and programmes different from, and reputedly better than, those put out by the commercial networks. The market for DBS in the States is understandable in view of the deplorable TV signal which is deflected by the number of high steel-frame buildings - and in view of the mediocre quality of the bulk of the network programmes. A company like Home Box Office, which is controlled by Warner Brothers, the film company, was bound to find subscribers, if only among viewers who wished to see feature films that were not constantly and arbitrarily interrupted by commercials. However, subscribers must have a gadget fitted to their sets to enable them to unscramble the Home Box Office signal, which is otherwise unintelligible.

In Britain the first DBS transmissions will begin in 1986. In this case it is not commercial interests which will be first in the field. The BBC has been offered access to two satellite channels: Channel 5 and Channel 6. Channel 5 will, in the somewhat clumsy formulation of a BBC executive, offer 'a service comprising mainly newly released films, but offer it much earlier than would normally be available to the basic network viewer'. A British version of Home Box Office, in fact. Channel 6 will be taken up with mixed programming including 'the best of international television', international news and repeats of British programming 'past and present'. These programmes will naturally not be had for nothing. The satellite alone will cost £168 million, to which must be added the cost of leasing the two channels at £12 million a piece, plus the cost of programmes. The sum of £100 a year has been mentioned, but seems low; to that must be added the cost of the antenna or the fee for the supply of the signal from a more remote antenna by a cable operator. From the point of view of the BBC the prospect of being able to supplement its licence revenue has obvious attractions. It could make the BBC slightly less dependent on the government for permission to increase the licence fee, although such aspirations towards independence are not likely to be encouraged in the present political climate. What has to be pointed out is that in proposing to charge a sum supplementary to the licence - a sum which will automatically cut out very large groups in society (including many pensioners, the unemployed and those on supplementary benefit), the BBC is proposing to introduce two-tier television: one television for the rich and the other for the rest of the population.

Cable and DBS alike represent a break with an important tradition in British broadcasting: it is the tradition of public service broadcasting. Historically, it owes its origins to the vague Fabianism which was current in certain political circles and even in some parts of the civil service after the First World War. An example of the importance of this strain of thought is to be found in the career of Sir Stephen Tallents, who as a civil servant during the war worked on rationing with Beveridge, the man who was to draw up the plan that bears his name and is the foundation stone of the Welfare State. Tallents's wartime experiences convinced him that profit was not always just or efficient. Still as a civil servant, Tallents went on to encourage the rise of British documentary film-making by employing John Grierson first at the Empire Marketing Board and later at the GPO Film Unit. He subsequently became the first head of public relations for the BBC. Here Sir John Reith was in charge, a curiously compounded personality who combined deference to authority with a certain professional radicalism and stubbornness. He, too, was of the opinion that the profit motive was not the only mainspring of human action. As first Director General of the BBC he was dedicated to the concept of broadcasting as a non-profit-making public service accessible to anyone who had paid the legally necessary licence fee - no matter where that person lived (unlike commercial TV - see pages 66-67).

The concept of public service is threatened by the exclusiveness of 'two-tier' broadcasting. What is perhaps even more worrying is that if viewers pay for DBS there is no good reason in economic logic why they should not also pay for normal transmissions. In an era when public enterprises are being handed back to private profit, why should broadcasting be exempt? After all, the BBC makes considerable profits, which are ploughed back into broadcasting, from its BBC Enterprises division, which deals with sales of programmes and merchandising. The present Director General of the BBC is on record as saying that the BBC will not necessarily last for ever. Can the possibility be excluded that radical conservatism, which is what Thatcherism has represented, might, for doctrinal and political reasons, move towards ending public service broadcasting, using as its weapons the new technologies of cable and DBS and the arguments of the market-place?

In this situation - even if the scenario presented above should prove unnecessarily alarmist - the left has to consider the extent to which (if at all) the concept of public service should be defended and used as a weapon against the commercial and political pressures which have become apparent in recent years, and which were exemplified by the government's treatment of the broadcasting institutions during the Falklands War.

11 In Defence of Public Broadcasting

The Reithean tradition in broadcasting is bound up with certain concepts which have been built into the ideology and the practice of both the BBC and the IBA. They include the concept of consensual broadcasting, which is the expression of the view that there is in our society broad agreement on a number of fundamental topics - politics, religion, sex, economics - and that views lying within the consensus will receive air-time as a matter of course, while views that lie outside the consensus will be excluded except in somewhat unusual circumstances. When they are allowed expression, they are clearly labelled as extreme, deviant, non-consensual, and in effect are marginalised; those who express them are treated as oddities. Since the advent of Channel 4 there have been some attempts to allow voices to be heard which are not normally represented - voices of ethnic minorities, of women and of young people; but it is in the nature of Channel 4 that such programmes are ghettos within a ghetto. Nevertheless, their mere presence is deeply disturbing to conservative critics of the channel.

In normal times, the consensual model allows the broadcasters to operate comfortably. An institution like the BBC keeps a tally of politicians and other spokespersons. When complaints are made it can demonstrate that over a period of time - several months - a balance between right and left has been preserved (these terms being employed within the limits of the parliamentary spectrum). It is true that, in terms of news coverage, the party in power receives more day-to-day coverage than the opposition; but when members of the opposition complain, they are confronted with the assurance that if they come to power they will be equally favoured. Within the consensus there is a genuine debate in the sense that in normal times it is assumed that there are two sides to every question - a 'right-wing' and a 'left-wing' view - and that the main parties contain a similar balance between left and right. Or such at least was the simple model until the arrival of the SDP and the Alliance, which has to be accommodated. The SDP owed much of its publicity in its early days to the broadcast media, partly, one suspects, because its political stance coincides with the middle-of-the-road position of many broadcasting executives; partly because of the disenchantment of many broadcasting executives with the old parties and their pressures. However that may be, the principle of consensual broadcasting - which still obtains despite the complicating factor of the SDP - is that all important questions (and others of less than national importance, in local politics, for instance) can be treated with evenhandedness. There is View A which is challenged by View B. Both are aired and the viewers are left to draw their own conclusions from the debate. Of course, the debate is not usually very extensive and is determined in its terms and its coverage by the interviewer or chairperson who sets the agenda and controls the situation. It would be wrong to suggest that it is always easy for the broadcasters to operate within the consensus; they are frequently criticised by politicians for suspected lack of balance. However, the institutions are highly skilled at answering such criticisms. A disgruntled politician can often be quietened by an invitation to take part in a studio discussion.

What is important is that since the Second World War (when there was no question of balance in the sense it has been discussed above and no debate even on matters of social and political importance like the Beveridge Plan was allowed), evenhandedness has come to be regarded by the broadcasters, and in particular those working in the news and current affairs, as an unchallenged doctrine. The Falklands War demonstrated that this was by no means the case.

It was suddenly no longer possible for the BBC, for instance, to suggest that there was a British point of view on the crisis and an Argentinian one - and that both should be presented to the public, which would make up its own mind. *Newsnight* came under attack for suggesting that this was the case, as did *Panorama* for a programme which featured Conservative 'wets', who were not 100 per cent behind Thatcher. As the Defence Committee Report on the handling of press and publication information during the Falklands conflict puts it:

On a number of occasions the Prime Minister and other

Government ministers criticised the media, particularly the BBC, for unbalanced and irresponsible reporting of the preparations for, and conduct of, the campaign. For example, on 11 May 1982 at Question Time, the Prime Minister said that 'I know how strongly people feel that the case of our country is not being put with sufficient vigour on certain - I do not say all - BBC programmes.'

What in fact Thatcher was complaining about was the concept of evenhandedness and, beyond that, the possibility of criticism of government policy and government actions in time of war. To put it another way, the professional practice of the broadcasters came into conflict with the political will of the government. It was a situation which presented the BBC and the IBA - more particularly ITN and the current affairs editors in the ITV companies - with difficult decisions.

The BBC had been in this situation once before - at the time of the Suez crisis and the Anglo-French-Israeli invasion of Egypt. At that time there was, according to reliable sources close to top management in the BBC, a proposal by the government of the day, under Prime Minister Eden, to commandeer the BBC's Overseas Services, broadcasting to listeners abroad in English and a great many other languages. The root of governmental dissatisfaction then was that in its Overseas Services the BBC had decided that both sides of the debate - which was being conducted fiercely in the press and elsewhere - should be openly expressed. Evenhandedness, in this case, included reviews of the British press. The management of the Overseas Services, supported by central management in Broadcasting House, decided to stick to its practices and policy in defiance of the government of the day. This resolve was made in the light of political judgements about the balance of forces in the Houses of Parliament, in the press and in influential sections of the establishment, not all of whom were enthusiastic about the invasion. In the event, the government backed down from a confrontation and limited itself to the attachment of a Foreign Office official to the Overseas Services, where he was easily marginalised by the BBC executives. In the case of the Falklands, the BBC did not resist.

This is not to say that the decision to fall in line took place without a long and wide-ranging debate. Like most important decisions in the field of politics and current affairs, the scope of the discussion is reflected in the minutes of the most important policy-making body in this area: the weekly meeting chaired by the Editor of News and Current Affairs (ENCA). During the crisis, this meeting was sometimes attended by the Director General in his capacity as editor-in-chief or by his designated successor. Part of the debate hinged on the question of whether the BBC could be independent in the sense of running contrary to what was perceived as being the 'mood of the nation'. Whether the forces committed to the war should be described as the 'British' forces or 'our' forces became the focus of conflict. The first formulation clearly suggests that there is some point of detachment from which British and Argentinian forces could be impartially observed; the second is an expression of patriotic commitment. The discussion, which centred on the nature of public opinion, was naturally to some extent a circular one, for the media play an essential role in shaping public opinion and then, by reflecting it, confirm opinions and attitudes which they have inculcated. What appears to have happened in the case of the Falklands War is that the broadcasters were outstripped by the press - and in particular the popular press - in its identification with what was interpreted as a surge of patriotism. The attacks on the BBC which followed - in particular by the most wildly jingoistic papers - clearly demonstrated that the old animosity between Fleet Street and the BBC is by no means dead. One of the reasons for the government's annoyance was the fact that in such moments of crisis the public turns in large numbers to the broadcasting media for information, their news services and current affairs programmes being seen as less obviously biased than the press. Thus LWT's Sunday morning programme *Weekend World* increased its audience by something close to 60 per cent, to 1.7 million. The pressures for the broadcasters to conform to the point of view of the government, or what the government saw as the national point of view, were therefore very strong.

The question which poses itself is whether the BBC could have stood out against the government and pursued an 'independent' point of view on the war. It has been argued that the broadcasting institutions were, in the words of the Television Act, 'duly objective' and 'duly impartial' - but not absolutely. That is to say, they were as objective and as impartial as circumstances allowed. This somewhat casuistical argument is valid only if it is assumed that centralised broadcasting institutions are, in the last resort, unable to assert their traditional 'independence'. (Reith took a similar view of the degree of liberty of action permitted to the BBC by his behaviour during the General Strike.) The alternative would have been for the BBC to assert its independence, to pursue a policy of evenhandedness and to continue to deal with the problem presented by Edward Heath who, before vanishing for the duration of the conflict, made a brief appearance and challenged the government to explain why it had turned down the Peruvian peace formula. Instead, the BBC fell in with the 'mood of the nation' as presented by the other media, and busied itself 'counting them out and counting them in' without any detached critical appraisal of the conduct of the campaign. It would be difficult, for instance, to deduce from the television coverage of the war that there are military men who are extremely critical of the whole Colonel H episode, which they believe was a bungled operation under a commanding officer who did not sufficiently trust his subordinates, had no right to be where he was and, by his death, cost the nation a very large sum of money in the shape of its investment in his training. It may well be that an assertion of 'independence' would have led to an outright attack on the BBC. In this context, it has to be remembered that the government can, in theory (and once threatened to) sack the Board of Governors - and might have done precisely that unless the governors had already taken action themselves in getting rid of the Director General. But this is an unlikely scenario.

The truth of the matter is that, among the BBC staff and among its reporters, there were those who were as happy as some press journalists to be able to cast off 'objectivity', although not all of them were as explicit about their joy at losing their chains as Max Hastings of the *Evening Standard*. The attitude of the senior editors involved towards government censorship of news shows how easily professional norms could be abandoned. It has long been the convention with news film originating from a country which censors outgoing material to alert viewers to this fact by superimposing a caption saying 'censored' on the screen. In the case of the Falklands War there was no such warning, although all film was censored and held up for long periods. The editor of ITN has since admitted on the air that perhaps, with hindsight, this was a mistake. The point remains: during the conflict there was no clear indication to the public of the way in which the news was being controlled and managed. On the other hand, Argentinian film, which was available throughout, was treated with automatic scepticism. This was arguably necessary because material originated under a dictatorship which has a close grip on news sources. But Argentinian film was presented as being necessarily mendacious; no real attempt was made to examine it and determine its validity as evidence. The Glasgow Media Group, which produced *Bad News* and its subsequent additions, has done work on the use of Argentinian film. This clearly demonstrates that in those cases where the film does tell the truth (why should the junta conceal genuine successes?) the ITN and BBC commentaries attempt to prove that it is lying. Cases in point concern the operational state of the Port Stanley air-strip at a time when British sources were saying that it was usable at most by light planes. In this case, the visual evidence on film that it was being used by large transports was simply brushed aside. The second case concerns the shooting down of a Hawker fighter, wreckage of which was clearly identifiable. Here, an attempt was made to suggest that there was a lot of wreckage about and the plane could not be identified with certainty.

It is extremely difficult to decide to what extent such lack of 'objectivity' is the result of editorial pressures; to what extent it is due to the interpretation by sub-editors of institutional policy as it has filtered down to them; or to what extent it reflects the general attitude prevalent in the newsroom at the time. It would certainly require a good deal of courage for a sub-editor to take a stand on the interpretation of a piece of enemy newsfilm in a situation where the institution as a whole had decided to go along with the 'national mood' and the desires of the government. Even in retrospect - that is to say in the cassettes put out subsequently by both the BBC and the ITN of Falklands coverage - there is no attempt at a critical historical appraisal of the war. These are celebratory tapes in which news footage is presented in a way that gives it the gloss and rhythm of feature film. The Falklands tapes are not by any stretch of the imagination either evenhanded or 'objective'.

Other problems raised by the Falklands War have a less direct bearing on the broadcasting institutions. They concern the problem of misinformation. According to the Defence Committee Report

> Many principles supposedly regarded as sacred and absolute within the media, are applied in a less rigid and categorical way by the public as a whole when it is judging its Government's conduct of a war. In our judgement the public is, in general, *quite ready to tolerate being misled to some extent* if the enemy is also

misled, thereby contributing to the success of the campaign [my emphasis].

This is clearly a very important and somewhat frightening statement even though it is qualified by the comment that no government would seek, 'in its urgent need to prosecute a war successfully, to insulate itself from the process of democratic accountability'. How would this apply, one cannot but wonder, in the run-up to a nuclear war?

There were some journalists - notably the defence correspondent of *The Economist* who argued that 'it can never be right for a democratic government to seek to use the free press as an organ of misinformation'. This view was not shared by the committee. The voice of the broadcasting institutions has not been heard publicly on this topic, although they have very properly criticised the obstructions placed in the way of getting pictures back from the scene of the operation. What is even more remarkable than the government's manipulation of the news, however, is the fact that foreign broadcasting organisations were excluded from covering events. CBS news in London was reduced to interviewing the clients of cafes and restaurants in the vicinity of its West End offices. The predictable results were relayed to the United States as some sort of accurate reflection of British public opinion. The point about foreign media coverage is that those involved would not have felt the need to respond to public jingoism or to accept the government line uncritically. The tenor of foreign media coverage of Northern Ireland is strikingly different from that of the BBC or ITV. Unfortunately, there is not in this country anything corresponding to the American First Amendment, which guaranteed freedom of information even during the Vietnam War (a freedom, it should be said, which did not preclude notable examples of self-censorship by indigenous television networks).

The Falklands War is important to a discussion of the British broadcasting institutions because it raises in a concrete way the questions of independence, of objectivity and of even-handedness - all three being terms which are central to the ideology of the broadcasters. There can be little doubt that a radical Conservative government, given a prolonged period in power, will attempt to limit the freedoms of the broadcasters by applying pressures both public and private. The institutions will make a judgement of the situation and adapt their responses to their reading of it. What the left has to address itself to when considering the media is the question of whether there is anything in the Reithean tradition of public service broadcasting which is worth defending or of developing in the face of such an attack, of a swing to the right and a situation where jingoism, economic crisis, unemployment and Conservative radicalism come together. It is a conjuncture that has sombre models in the past and one that fully justifies Tony Benn's description of Thatcher's policies as 'benign fascism'. Is there, for instance, a case for supporting a call for greater independence on the part of the broadcasting institutions? Are there forces within those institutions which would welcome external support in fighting for such independence in a campaign which took at face value the old familiar formulations about 'independence', 'objectivity' and professional codes. Is there a political case to be made for a more representative form of control over the institutions?

One of the difficulties which has been encountered in the past in proposing such a debate has been the indifference, and indeed the ignorance, of politicians and of activists on the left about the media. If nothing else, the Falklands War has brought home the importance of the subject to many people who were previously indifferent or sceptical about the debates conducted, usually in academic circles, about the effects and social function of broadcasting. The Falklands War posed the problem concretely and urgently. But, by extension, it also poses the problem of the place of broadcasting in society. There is a view which is sometimes described as pessimistic, but which others consider merely realistic. This states that in any society - capitalist or socialist - public broadcasting institutions must perforce reflect a consensus and conduct debates within it. It is difficult to believe that a socialist society, for instance, would encourage the broadcasting of ideas aimed at the destruction of that society - which is the reason why radical and revolutionary ideas are kept off the air or ghettoised in our late-capitalist one. This has been described as an illiberal attitude. But the point is precisely that it is not possible to discuss broadcasting, which is closely bound up with politics and with political control, in terms of a vague liberalism. It is, however, possible to say that certain concepts elaborated under a liberal regime - like the concepts of evenhandedness, of independence, etc. - should be defended against the right-wing attacks in the same way as freedom of speech and trade union rights must be defended. But beyond that are more fundamental questions relating to the place of broadcasting in society and of the controls society places upon it. To suggest that technological developments will lead to an easy utopian solution to those questions is to evade and avoid the issue, which might be formulated in these terms: In a socialist society how much freedom should be granted to broadcasters? To what extent should they be allowed to be 'independent' and therefore free to criticise developments in society? How far should pluralism be allowed to flourish? Trotsky, describing the early days of the Bolshevik Party, talks of the amount of debate and discussion that went on. How can that freedom be preserved and what part should the media play in it? Hans Magnus Enzensberger has suggested that the media are by their nature 'dirty'. By this he means that they are subject to manipulation (in the literal sense of the word) whereby images and words are put together to make statements. Furthermore, there is a wider sense of media's manipulation which involves their expression of ideologies within society. Enzensberger's appeal for those who concern themselves with the media to come to terms with this problem is still valid - increasingly and dangerously so in the present climate of political reaction.

Suggestions for further reading

Your local library should be able to obtain any book on this list without difficulty.

Asa Briggs, *The History of Broadcasting in the United Kingdom*, London, Oxford University Press, Vol. 1 1961; Vol. 2 1965, Vol. 4 1979. A full and well-documented account which relies heavily on official sources. See, in particular, Vol. 3 1979, *Sound and Vision*, for the beginnings of television.

Anthony Smith, *British Broadcasting*, Newton Abbott, David and Charles, 1974. A good source book which quotes from important documents in the history of the media.

Charles Stuart (editor), *The Reith Diaries*, London, Collins, 1975. Fascinating material from the personal diaries of the founder of the BBC and of British broadcasting.

Grace Wyndam Goldie, *Facing the Nation: Television and Politics 1936-76*, London, Bodley Head, 1977. A first-hand account by a distinguished pioneer of political broadcasting of the relationship of the BBC to political power.

Tom Burns, *The BBC: Public Institution and Private World*, London, Macmillan, 1977. An important sociological account of how the BBC works.

Lord Hill (Charles Hill), *Behind The Screen: The Broadcasting Memoirs of Lord Hill of Luton*, London, Sidgwick and Jackson, 1974. An account of British broadcasting by a politician who was chairman of the ITA and then of the BBC.

Stanley Cohen and Jock Young (editors), *The Manufacture of News: Social Problems, Deviance and the Mass Media*, London, Constable, 1973. A good collection of essays - see especially Stuart Hall on 'A world at one with itself'.

Philip Schlesinger, *Putting 'Reality' Together*, BBC News, London, Constable, 1978. An analysis of BBC news.

Glasgow Media Group, *Bad News* and *More Bad News*, London, Routledge and Kegan Paul, 1976 and 1980 respectively. A detailed and important analysis of such topics as 'newstalk', the framing of news pictures and the treatment of industrial disputes on television.

Peter Beharrell and Greg Philo (editors), *Trade Unions and the Media*, London, Macmillan, 1977. Interesting essays on how trade unions are presented on the air.

Manuel Alvarado and Edward Buscombe, *Hazell: The Making of a TV Series*, London, BFI/Latimer, 1978. Television as an industry illustrated from the production processes involved in making a popular series.

Anthony Smith, *The Geopolitics of Information*, London, Faber & Faber, 1980. A lucid description of the domination of the media by the developed countries.

Jeremy Tunstall, *The Media are American: Anglo-American Media in the World*, London, Constable, 1977. Another study of the same problem.

Herbert Schiller, *Mass Communications and American Empire*, New York, Angustin M. Kelley, 1970. A marxist contribution to the problem of media domination.

Raymond Williams, *Television: Technology and Cultural Form*, London, Fontana/Collins, 1974. One of the outstanding theorists and historians of the media examines the relationship of technology to social change.

Open University (publisher) Course Units
The following units are useful and accessible: Unit One: *Issues in the Study of Mass Communications*; Unit Ten: *Patterns of Ownership*; Unit Thirteen: *The Media as Definers of Social Reality*.

British Film Institute (publisher) Television Monographs. The following monographs published in this series are informed, clear and cheap: Richard Collins, *Television News*, 1976; Caroline Heller, *Broadcasting and Accountability*, 1978; Charlotte Brunsdon and David Morley, *Everyday Television: Nationwide*, 1978; Nicolas Garnham (2nd ed.), *Structures of Television*, 1978.

Denis MacShane, *Using the Media*, London, Pluto Press, 1979. A useful account of how to deal with the media.

Report of the Committee on Broadcasting 1960, Cmnd. 1753, HMSO, London, 1960. The 'Pilkington Report'. *Report of the Committee on the Future of Broadcasting 1977*, Cmnd. 6753, HMSO, London, 1977. The 'Annan Report'. Both these reports are valuable in that they give clear accounts of the history and organisation of the broadcast institutions in Britain and of their finances and performance. Both are well written and readable.

Paul Sieghart (editor), *Micro-chips with Everything*, London, Comedia Publisher Group, 1982. A series of debates at the Institute of Contemporary Arts on the consequences of information technology.

Stephen Lambert, *Channel Four, Television with a Difference*, London, BFI, 1982. An interesting account of the lead-up to Channel 4 which çovers the history of ITV and the debate around the new channel.

Brian Wenham (editor), *The Third Age of Broadcasting*, London, Faber & Faber, 1982. A bland look at the future which gives interesting insights into the minds of the organisation men (no women contributors).

Report of the Inquiry into Cable Expansion and Broadcasting Policy, Cmnd. 8679, London, HMSO, 1982. Lord Hunt's mild report, opening the door to the cable entrepreneurs. Repays study in terms of its language and assumptions.

Useful organisations

**Advertising Standards
Authority**
2-16 Torrington Place
London WC1
01 580 5555

**Black Media Workers'
Association**
29c Lanhill Road
London W9

**Campaign for Press and
Broadcasting Freedom**
9 Poland Street
London W1 3DG
01 437 2795

**Campaign against Racism
in the Media**
PO Box 50
London N1

Channel 4 Users Group
9 Poland Street
London W1 3DG

Community Radio Association
c/o 92 Huddleston Road
London N7 0EG
01 263 6692

Free the Airwaves
Box CCR
c/o The Bath House
Gwydir Street
Cambridge

Glasgow University Media Group
Dept of Sociology
University of Glasgow
61 Southpark Ave
Glasgow G12
041 339 8855

Local Radio Workshop
12 Praed Mews
London W2
01 402 7651

London Media Research Group
30 Granville Square
London WC1
01 278 3857

Women in Media
BM WIM
London WC1N 3XX

**Women's Media Action
Group (formerly AFFIRM)**
c/o A Woman's Place
48 William IV Street
London WC2

**Women's Monitoring
Network**
c/o AWP
48 William IV Street
London WC2